Girls talk

An anti-stigma program for young women

to promote understanding of

and awareness about depression

A participatory action research and development project

of the VALIDITY ♀ team

FACILITATOR'S MANUAL

Girls Talk mission statement

The Girls Talk program provides a safe place for young women to connect with each other and to learn about depression and its contributing factors. Young women will develop self-awareness, coping strategies and critical thinking skills through artistic and recreational activities.

camh
Centre for Addiction and Mental Health
Centre de toxicomanie et de santé mentale

© 2009 CAMH

Girls Talk: An anti-stigma program for young women to promote
understanding of and awareness about depression

Facilitator's manual

ISBN: 978-1-77052-398-2 (PRINT)
ISBN : 978-1-77052-399-9 (PDF)
ISBN : 978-1-77052-400-2 (HTML)
ISBN : 978-1-77052-401-9 (ePUB)
Product code: PG 137

Suggested citation:
VALIDITY ♀ team, CAMH. (2009). *Girls Talk: An Anti-Stigma Program for
Young Women to Promote Understanding of and Awareness about Depression.
Facilitator's Manual.* Toronto: Centre for Addiction and Mental Health.

This publication may be available in other formats. For information about
alternate formats or other CAMH publications, or to place an order, please
contact Sales and Distribution:

Toll-free: 1 800 661-1111
Toronto: 416 595-6059
E-mail: publications@camh.net
Online store: http://store.camh.net

Website: www.camh.net

4058/10-2009 PG 137

CONTENTS

ACKNOWLEDGMENTS

This guide was created by a team of vibrant women who want to empower adolescent girls to build resilience within themselves. We want to extend gratitude to all the people who have helped develop the Girls Talk program and this facilitator's guide.

LEAD AUTHOR
Cathy Thompson

CONTRIBUTING AUTHORS
Pam Gillett, Angela Martella

FOCUS GROUPS
Youth Net Halton and Youth
    Net/Réseau Ado Ottawa

REVIEWERS
Kim Baker, CAMH
Merryl Bear, National Eating Disorder
    Information Centre
Fran Buchanan, Hamilton Family
    Health Team
Katie Cino, Youth Net Halton
Karen Degagne, Youth Net/Réseau
    Ado Ottawa
Jennifer Minn, For You Telecare Family
    Service, North York
Monica Nunes, CAMH
Michelle Petersen, Youth Net/Réseau
    Ado Ottawa
Neena Riarh, Region of Peel Health
    Department

PRODUCT DEVELOPMENT
Julia Greenbaum, Cathy Thompson,
    CAMH

EDITORIAL
Nick Gamble, Kelly Coleman, CAMH

DESIGN
Nancy Leung, CAMH

PRINT PRODUCTION
Chris Harris, CAMH

TYPESETTING
Laura Brady

We extend a huge "thank you" to the
VALIDITY♀ team and all the past
participants in the Girls Talk program
for their commitment to this initiative.

A NOTE FOR SERVICE PROVIDERS

The Girls Talk program was created in response to an overwhelming need for adolescent girls to have a safe space to connect and share with one another. Although the program is comprehensive, there is no single fit for all groups, so we encourage you to tailor the program to the needs of the girls in your group. Empower them to understand how Girls Talk can increase their resilience and coping skills. Above all else, have fun! We thank you for your time and commitment to Girls Talk.

Sincerely,
CAMH Members of the VALIDITY ♀ Team
www.camh.net/validity

PART 1
Introduction to Girls Talk

What is Girls Talk?

Girls Talk is an eight-session anti-stigma program for girls, generally between the ages of 13 and 16. The focus is on preventing depression and educating the girls about depression. The program is not intended for those who have been diagnosed with or are in treatment for depression.

The Girls Talk program has evolved as part of a larger project called VALIDITY ♀ (Vibrant Action Looking Into Depression In Today's Young Women), a participatory action research project aimed at increasing understanding of factors that lead to depression in young women, and developing strategies, materials and interventions to address these factors.

Throughout the process of developing and implementing the activities in VALIDITY ♀, young women were actively involved in positions of leadership, including leading focus groups in communities across Ontario to gather information from peers and service providers about depression and young women, and planning a provincial conference in Windsor in 2001.

The main theme that emerged from this process was the need for a safe space where girls could be themselves and not have to deal with the unrelenting pressures of adolescence and daily life. The girls stressed the need for a supportive environment in which they could share their feelings with other girls without fear of negative comments or ridicule. They recognized that the stigma of mental illness is a huge barrier to getting help. They also described a need to strengthen self-esteem; to understand ways to develop meaningful relationships; to understand the influence of the media on young women; and to educate parents, teachers and service providers about depression and about how they can help.

Based on the findings from the focus groups and the conference, and recommendations from the VALIDITY♀ Youth Action team, the Girls Talk program was created by the Centre for Addiction and Mental Health (CAMH). In keeping with the model of youth involvement, CAMH partnered with Youth Net/Réseau Ado in Ottawa and the Youth Net Program in Halton to pilot the Girls Talk program in spring 2004. The program was so well received that both organizations continue to include it as part of their core programming. CAMH recognizes the ongoing need for this type of girls' program and has taken the lead in updating and disseminating this facilitator's guide to make it accessible for organizations across Canada.

Literature review

There is a wide body of clinical and empirical literature* that describes adolescence as a particularly vulnerable time for females (e.g., Marcotte et al., 2002; Manion et al., 1997). Research shows that beginning in early adolescence, girls are more stressed than boys (Colton & Gore, 1991), more depressed (Marcotte et al., 2002; Nolen-Hoeksema & Girgus, 1994), have lower self-esteem (Chubb et al., 1997), have more eating disorders (Croll et al., 2002), and more body dissatisfaction (Brumberg, 1997; Harter, 2000). Gilligan et al. (1990) described adolescence as a time when girls "lose their voice," experiencing a diminished confidence in their ability to express their needs and opinions. Thus there is consistent evidence that during adolescence, girls experience a decline in mental health and well-being that often persists through adulthood.

A review of the prevention and treatment literature with regard to adolescent girls reveals that programs tend to be problem-specific; that is, they are designed to reduce particular symptoms. Findings from studies examining the effectiveness of these programs show mixed results. This has led to a call for programs that target general factors, rather than symptom-specific behaviours (Shisslak & Crago, 2001). For example, Striegel-Moore & Cachelin (1999) state that strong coping skills and self-efficacy can act as protective factors against

* We thank Dr. Donna Akman of CAMH for providing this literature review.

mental health problems. Turner (1995) writes that self-esteem and self-efficacy may be the most important traits in resilient people. In fact, self-esteem has been identified as a buffer against a variety of stressors (Statistics Canada, 2003). According to the findings of a longitudinal National Population Health Survey (Statistics Canada, 2003) a weak self-concept, as indicated by poor self-esteem and poor sense of mastery, was predictive of depression among girls. Furthermore, having a weak self-concept tended to put girls at risk of poor self-perceived health and obesity. These findings led to the conclusion that a strong self-concept appears to be a key factor in developing good mental and physical health (Statistics Canada, 2003).

The use of female-only groups is considered an ideal setting for these programs. Relational theories of women's psychological development emphasize the importance of connections among girls and women (Gilligan, 1992; Gilligan et al., 1990). All-girl groups may promote these connections to a degree that mixed-gender groups will not (Chaplin et al., 2006).

Developmental assets

The foundation of the Girls Talk program is building resilience in young women. The Search Institute (a U.S. non-profit organization that promotes positive change on behalf of young people) lists 40 "developmental assets" that young people need in order to grow up healthy, caring and responsible. Girls Talk encompasses many of these assets, both internal and external.

Among the external assets, Girls Talk addresses *support*, *empowerment*, *boundaries and expectations*, and *constructive use of time*. The girls in the program have an opportunity to learn from caring adults in their school or community and are exposed to different learning mediums, including the physical and the artistic. The participants also learn from each other and form connections that empower them to face challenges in their lives.

The Girls Talk program also builds girls' capacity to develop more internal assets. Specifically, *positive identity* is greatly boosted by participating in the program. The program increases girls' ability to focus on their own *personal power*, *self-esteem* and *sense of purpose*. At the end of the program, the facilitators encourage the participants to think about having a *positive view of their personal future*.

For more information about the Developmental Assets framework, visit the Search Institute website at www.search-institute.org/assets.

Program overview

OBJECTIVES

After completing the Girls Talk program, it is expected that the participants will demonstrate their understanding of depression: potential causes, symptoms and treatment options. The girls will gain an understanding of the interrelation between depression and self-esteem, body image, stress, relationships and the media. They will also build on their skills to cope with daily life events.

ABOUT THE PROGRAM

The Girls Talk program comprises activities that are experiential, actively involving the participants in physical, artistic and intellectual ways. A substantial discussion component is included to give the girls an opportunity to connect on a personal level and to discuss issues that are important to them.

Girls Talk consists of eight weekly sessions of between 90 and 120 minutes each. The program is facilitated by two professionals who have a background in working with young women and who are youth friendly.

COMPONENTS

Each Girls Talk session includes the following components:
• education about a predetermined topic related to depression
• a group discussion
• an activity (artistic or physical)
• journal writing.

The topics covered during the sessions were determined through the VALIDITY♀ project (from the voices of young women) and through research about factors influencing young women and depression. They include depression, stigma, stress, relationships, self-esteem, media and body image.

THE FACILITATORS

The facilitators are integral to the success of the Girls Talk program. They act as mentors, bringing out the strengths in the girls who participate. As well as conducting the sessions, facilitators are responsible for reviewing the lesson plans before the sessions, ensuring there are adequate food and supplies, and completing any required forms.

Facilitators can be any youth-friendly professionals familiar with working in a school or community setting. Typically facilitators have been trained discussion group facilitators, social workers, teachers, guidance counsellors, practicum students or university student volunteers. The main qualities required of facilitators are:

- active listening skills
- good organizational skills
- experience working with young people
- experience facilitating groups of young people.

It is also helpful for facilitators to reflect the diversity of the group.

A guest speaker is also a great option for the group: a guest talking about her experiences with depression is an effective way to decrease the stigma associated with mental health problems. It also allows the girls to ask questions and discuss depression in a casual environment. The key content and messages should include the speaker's experience with depression and the components of her recovery, along with the idea that there is hope for people with depression.

SUPPLIES AND FACILITIES

If possible, a specific room should be allocated for the program. It should be large and open, and provide enough space to run the program activities. Because of the sensitive nature of some discussions, it is best to find a room that offers some privacy (e.g., a room that another group is not using simultaneously).

Each session in the Girls Talk facilitator's guide contains a supply list. The supplies required for *all* sessions are food and refreshments, journals and pens.

BUDGET

The Girls Talk program can be implemented with a minimal budget. The main costs are for space to run the group, supplies and refreshments. In many communities, supplies can be found at a dollar store and food can be bought at a discount grocery store to save costs. Often schools or local community groups have space they will provide free or at minimal charge.

AWARDS AND REFRESHMENTS

Session 8 of this facilitator's guide includes a sample Certificate of Completion that can be given to girls who "graduate" from the program.

During the pilot phase of the Girls Talk program, girls mentioned that they enjoyed having food and refreshments available at each session, although this is not essential. Girls also said that they liked to have healthy foods that will nourish their mind and body (e.g., fruit, vegetables, whole wheat bagels).

BEFORE YOU BEGIN

The VALIDITY♀ project has developed two resources that complement this Girls Talk facilitator's guide:

- *Hear Me, Understand Me, Support Me: What Young Women Want You to Know about Depression* (2006), written by young women and service providers. This guide provides stories and resources recommended by young women for other young women and service providers. It also contains important information about the challenges young women encounter in today's society.
- "Let's Talk: I'm More Than What You See" (2008), a poster developed by young women to engage service providers in conversation about the issues in young women's lives that affect their overall health.

Both these resources are available free at www.camh.net/validity. Throughout this facilitator's guide, quotes and resources are provided from *Hear Me, Understand Me, Support Me* that can be used with participants. **We also suggest you order a free copy of the "Let's Talk" poster to be posted on the wall at the group,** to remind participants about the many factors in their lives that can affect their health.

Using the Girls Talk facilitator's guide

This facilitator's guide contains detailed plans for each session of the Girls Talk program, along with handouts and background information. Young women have been involved in the development of the guide as well as the program as a whole; their feedback has been invaluable.

The session plans follow a standard format that includes:
- an overview of the objectives
- the supplies needed for the session
- recommended resources
- the topic of discussion (with background information for facilitators)
- instructions for the activities
- the topic for the session's journal entry.

The sessions typically last between 1.5 and 2 hours. The amount of time needed for each activity is estimated in the session plans, but will vary depending on the interests of the group.

Under each issue for discussion, there are notes for the facilitators. It is not necessary to cover each point; rather, they are included as reference information.

You may want to leave 10 minutes at the beginning or end of each session to discuss issues that are currently on the minds of the girls in the group. This need has been raised by previous participants in Girls Talk groups.

Tips for facilitators

Facilitators, especially those who are new to the program, should read the session plans carefully in advance to see what preparation is required and how the resources they prepare will be used in the session. (Resource materials are used in almost every session.)

Please take the time to discuss with your co-facilitator who will do what and how you will manage the session. It is also a good idea to debrief after each session, so you can monitor how the partnership is working and get one another's reactions to how the program is going. Included on page 9 is a progress report template* to record your notes about the sessions. Although it is important to cover the objectives in each session, when working with young people some flexibility is required to adapt to their needs and age level.

In an appendix to this guide ("Queen D," page 93) we present responses to common questions about depression written by young women who have dealt with depression themselves. You can use this material in sessions or print it for the girls to read at home.

To help you evaluate the effectiveness of the Girls Talk program, this guide includes a reproducible pretest (for the girls to complete during Session 1) and post-test (to be completed during Session 8).

Updated information, activities and materials will be made available on the VALIDITY ♀ website at www.camh.net/validity. Please make sure to check back regularly for more information to complement your program.

---

* The form is adapted from one used at a Girls Talk program at For You Telecare Family Service in Toronto.

Girls Talk progress report

Facilitators: _____

Session date: _____ Session no.: _____

Questions to think about

GIRLS

- What was the attendance?
- How are the girls getting along with one another? Any conflicts, issues or areas of concern?
- How are girls responding to discussion and activities?
- Do you feel that the girls are learning?
- Likes? Dislikes?
- Positives? Negatives?

Comments:

GROUND RULES AND CONFIDENTIALITY

During the first session of a Girls Talk group, you will need to set ground rules, including rules of confidentiality. Discuss with the group what rules they would like to see, and the consequences for not following the rules the group decides on.

Confidentiality is important in this type of group. Let the participants know that any information discussed and collected during the sessions will be kept strictly confidential within the limits of the law. (If, for example, a participant tells you that she intends to harm herself or others, or that she or someone she knows under the age of 16 [in Ontario] is being harmed in some way, you must disclose this information to the proper authorities and should provide the participant with access to help.

DOS AND DON'TS OF WORKING WITH YOUNG WOMEN

This list—compiled from the comments of young women in the VALIDITY♀ team's resource *Hear Me, Understand Me, Support Me* (2006, p. 75)—will help to guide your work.

Do

Build a relationship with us first before you start talking about depression.

Ask us if we have been affected by any of these:
• discomfort with our body
• issues relating to food
• parental pressure
• family problems
• racial and cultural experiences
• peer pressure
• sexual relationships
• sexuality issues
• economic issues
• school experiences
• low levels of physical activity
• stress

- visible and/or invisible disabilities
- sibling rivalry
- loss of someone important to us
- strained friendships
- use of alcohol or other substances
- abusive relationships
- politics or things that we see or hear about on the news
- anything else unique to us and our situations.

Educate us about depression. Ask the young woman if she wants information on depression. If so, she can take away resources to look at and then give you answers about what you need to know, and then talk about it.

Give us information on other things besides medication that can help with depression.

Empower us.

Always check things out with us to make sure you understand what we mean!

Don't

Don't tell us you know what we're going through, because unless you've been there, you don't really know what we're going through.

Don't do for us, but guide us.

When asking questions about issues on your checklist, don't forget to look up from your paper. You need to get to know us, so there needs to be time to talk about the things on the list.

Don't just hand us a number to call. We need information about a referral and what will happen when we call.

Don't ask yes/no questions. You need to hear about my world.

Don't assume that I want my family involved.

Don't talk to me like I'm a child.

Don't judge me by the way I dress.

Don't reject me because I am expressing anger—it has meaning, it needs to be understood.

Recruiting participants

The Girls Talk program is intended for girls between 13 and 16 years of age (though the program has been implemented successfully with young women up to the age of 20). It is a prevention program, and as such is targeted to girls who have *not* already been identified as having depression. Each group should be small enough to allow everyone to take turns sharing, but large enough to capture a range of views and experiences: we recommend a maximum of 12 participants.

The following pages include two reproducible documents that will be useful for recruiting participants:
• an information sheet for parents or caregivers
• a sample recruitment flyer to give you ideas for creating your own.*

* The flyer is adapted from one used at a Girls Talk program at For You Telecare Family Service in Toronto.

Girls Talk: Information for parents and caregivers

What is Girls Talk?

Girls Talk is a program being offered at _____ (location) beginning on _____ (date). The eight-week program includes discussion and education about self-esteem, body image, relationships, dealing with stress, and factors that contribute to depression. The girls who participate will have an opportunity to express themselves through different artistic projects, journal writing and discussion groups. The main purpose of the group is to provide a supportive environment to increase the connections girls have among themselves.

How will Girls Talk benefit my daughter?

Girls Talk will allow your daughter to meet with other girls her age and discuss matters that are important to them. She will learn about positive physical, emotional and mental health and receive educational material about different topics. She will hear guest speakers and receive instruction in various artistic endeavours. She will learn healthy ways to cope with stress and ways to help a friend who may be feeling depressed.

Where did Girls Talk come from?

The Girls Talk program was created as a result of focus groups held with young women through the Centre for Addiction and Mental Health (CAMH). The young women wanted to have a forum to discuss issues that were important to them and to learn more about the prevention, causes and treatment of depression.

Questions?

If you have any questions about the Girls Talk program, please contact

facilitator: _____

phone: _____

e-mail: _____

Sample Girls Talk flyer

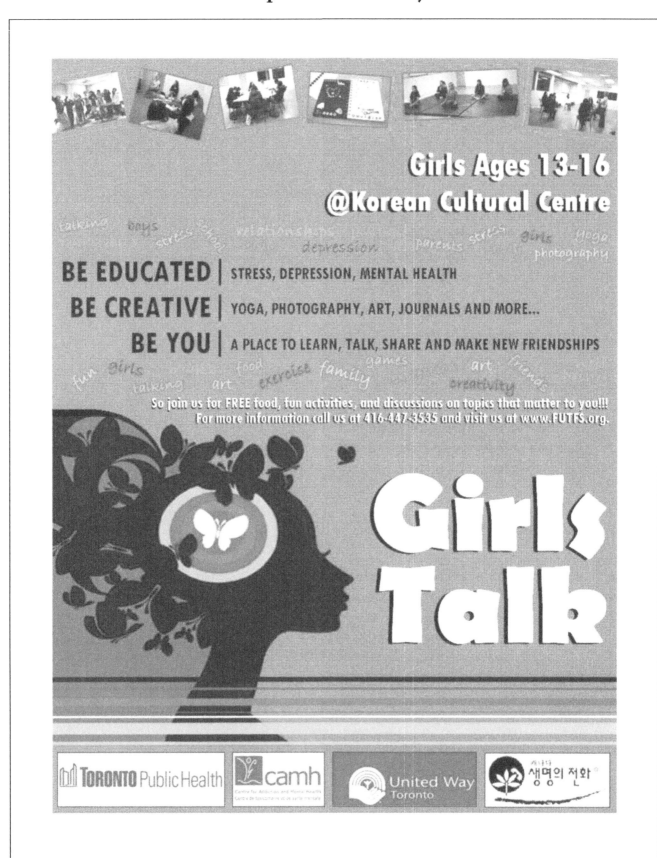

References

Brumberg, J.J. (1997). *The Body Project*. New York: Random House.

Chaplin, T., Gillham, J., Reivich, K., Elkon, A., Samuels, B., Freres, D. et al. (2006). Depression prevention for early adolescent girls: A pilot study of all-girls versus co-ed groups. *Journal of Early Adolescence, 26,* 110–126.

Chubb, N., Fertman, C. & Ross, J. (1997). Adolescent self-esteem and locus of control: A longitudinal study of gender and age differences. *Adolescence, 32* (125), 113–129.

Colton, M. & Gore, S., (1991). *Risk, Resiliency, and Resistance: Current Research on Adolescent Girls*. New York: Ms. Foundation.

Croll, J., Neumark-Stzainer, D., Story, M. & Ireland, M. (2002). Prevalence and risk and protective factors related to disordered eating behaviors among adolescents: Relationship to gender and ethnicity. *Journal of Adolescent Health, 31* (2), 166–175.

Gilligan, C. (1992). *In a Different Voice*. Cambridge, MA: Harvard University Press.

Gilligan, C., Lyons, N. & Hanmer, T. (Eds.). (1990). *Making connections*. Cambridge, MA: Harvard University Press.

Harter, S. (2000). Is self-esteem only skin-deep? The inextricable link between physical appearance and self-esteem. *Reclaiming Children and Youth, 9* (3), 133–138.

Manion, I.G., Davidson, S., Clark, S., Norris, C. & Brandon, S. (1997). Working with youth in the 1990s: Attitudes, behaviours, impressions and opportunities. *Canadian Psychiatric Association Bulletin, 29,* 111–114.

Marcotte, D., Fortin, L, Potvin, P. & Papillon, M. (2002). Gender differences in depressive symptoms during adolescence: Role of gender-typed characteristics, self-esteem, body image, stressful life events, and pubertal status. *Journal of Emotional and Behavioral Disorders, 10* (1), 29–42.

Nolen–Hoeksema, S. & Girgus, J. (1994). The emergence of gender differences in depression during adolescence. *Psychological Bulletin, 115,* 424–443.

Shisslak, C. & Crago, M. (2001). Risk and protective factors in the development of eating disorders. In J. Thompson & L. Smolak (Eds.), *Body Image, Eating Disorders and Obesity in Youth: Assessment, Prevention, and Treatment* (pp. 103–125). Washington, DC: American Psychological Association.

Statistics Canada. (2003). Adolescent self-concept and health into adulthood. *The Daily*, November 19. Available: www.statcan.ca/Daily/English/031119/d031119b.htm. Accessed July 30, 2009.

Striegel–Moore, R.H. & Cachelin, F.M. (1999). Body image concerns and disordered eating in adolescent girls: Risk and protective factors. In N.G. Johnson, M.C. Roberts & J. Worell (Eds.), *Beyond Appearance: A New Look at Adolescent Girls* (pp. 85–108). Washington, DC: American Psychological Association.

Turner, S., Norman, E. & Zunz, S. (1995). Enhancing resiliency in girls and boys: A case for gender specific adolescent prevention programming. *Journal of Primary Prevention, 16* (1), 25–38.

PART 2
Session-by-session guide

Overview of sessions

SESSION OUTLINES

Session 1: Introducing Girls Talk

OBJECTIVES

- Introduce the Girls Talk program and its goals, and give an overview of the eight sessions.
- Help the participants to get to know the other girls in the group.
- Fill out the required forms.
- Introduce the topics of mental health and depression.

ACTIVITIES

1. Introduction to Girls Talk and the eight sessions
2. Icebreaker: A little known fact
3. Paperwork: Commitment agreement and pretest
4. Activity: Skittles
5. Ground rules
6. Discussion: Girls' mental health
7. Introduction to journals

MATERIALS AND HANDOUTS

- flip chart and markers
- food
- CD or mp3 player, and music
- bowl of Skittles
- journals
- stickers and other craft supplies to decorate journals
- pens
- Handout 1A: Program Schedule
- Handout 1B: Commitment Agreement
- Handout 1C: Pretest
- fact sheet "The Facts about Teen Depression" (available from www.mooddisorders.on.ca/pdf/TeenDepression_final.pdf)

SESSION OUTLINES CONTINUED

Session 2: Stress

OBJECTIVES
- Discuss different causes of stress.
- Teach healthy ways to cope with stress and have the participants share their own coping strategies.
- Have the participants learn how stress affects girls' bodies by sharing their own experiences.
- Help the participants to understand how depression can arise out of a stressful situation and times of transition.

ACTIVITIES
1. Icebreaker: Stand up
2. Discussion: Stress
3. Activity: Stress and the body diagram
4. Activity: Yoga demonstration
5. Journal writing

MATERIALS AND HANDOUTS
- flip chart and markers
- food
- CD or mp3 player, and music
- pre-drawn outlines of a body on paper (enough copies for girls to work in pairs)
- pens
- yoga mats, gym mats or towels
- DVD player and yoga instruction DVD (or guest yoga instructor)

Session 3: Relationships with friends

OBJECTIVES
- Review the signs of healthy and unhealthy relationships.
- Remind the participants that everyone has the ability to be a good friend.
- Discuss how relationships can affect mental health.
- Discuss anger within relationships.

ACTIVITIES
1. Discussion: Relationships with friends
2. Activity: Personal attributes
3. Activity: Giving compliments and healing bracelets
4. Activity: Storytelling circle
5. Journal writing

MATERIALS AND HANDOUTS
- flip chart and markers
- food
- CD or mp3 player, and music
- scissors
- paper bag or other container
- small pieces of card, one envelope per girl
- healing bracelet supplies (beads, wire, etc.)
- pens
- Resource Sheet 3A: Personal Attributes
- Handout 3A: Colour Meanings and the Spectrum

SESSION OUTLINES CONTINUED

Session 4: Relationships with parents or caregivers

OBJECTIVES
- Review the qualities of healthy relationships.
- Discuss the impact of relationships with parents or caregivers, with respect to depression.
- Teach ways to effectively communicate and maintain positive relationships with parents or caregivers.

ACTIVITIES
1. Discussion: Healthy relationships
2. Discussion: Relationship with parents
3. Activity: Using "I" statements
4. Activity: Memory box
5. Journal writing

MATERIALS AND HANDOUTS
- food
- CD or mp3 player, and music
- boxes (one for each participant), decorative materials, glitter, stickers, scissors, glue
- pens
- Handout 4A: Communicating with Parents or Caregivers
- Handout 4B: Using "I" Statements
- Handout 4C: Feelings List

Session 5: Dating relationships

OBJECTIVES
- Discuss the impact of dating relationships on self-esteem and depression.
- Teach how to identify unhealthy relationships and how to get help.
- Discuss decision making within dating relationships.

ACTIVITIES
1. Discussion: Dating relationships
2. Activity: Dating violence facts
3. Discussion: Unhealthy or violent relationships
4. Activity: My rights for date nights
5. Journal writing

MATERIALS AND HANDOUTS
- food
- CD or mp3 player, and music
- stickers and markers
- tape and scissors
- pens
- Handout 5A: Power and Control Wheel
- Handout 5B: Equality Wheel
- Handout 5C: My Rights for Date Nights
- Resource Sheets 5A–5F: Dating Violence Facts

SESSION OUTLINES CONTINUED

Session 6: Self-esteem

OBJECTIVES
- Through discussion and creative work, encourage girls to build healthy and durable self-esteem.
- Explore the power of words.
- Discuss factors that can affect self-esteem.
- Discuss how self-esteem is related to depression.

ACTIVITIES
1. Icebreaker: What I like about being me
2. Discussion: Self-esteem
3. Activity: Inner critic vs. inner champion
4. Activity: Dancing
5. Activity: Thank-you card (optional)
6. Journal writing

MATERIALS AND HANDOUTS
- flip chart and markers
- food
- CD or mp3 player, and music
- DVD player and dance instruction DVD (or guest dance instructor)
- pens
- cards, lettering and markers to make thank-you cards (if choosing this optional activity)

Session 7: Body image and the media

OBJECTIVES
- Encourage the participants to critically examine how the media portray young women and help create distorted ideas of body image.
- Examine the relationship between images in the media and self-esteem.
- Brainstorm ways to promote a healthy body image.
- Discuss the links between body image and depression.

ACTIVITIES
1. Discussion: Body image and the media
2. Activity: Magazine collage
3. Activity: Challenging negative media messages
4. Journal writing

MATERIALS AND HANDOUTS
- flip chart and markers
- food
- CD or mp3 player, and music
- a selection of women's magazines
- bristol board (one piece for every two or three girls)
- scissors, glue, tape, markers
- computer with Internet connection (optional)
- pens

SESSION OUTLINES CONTINUED

Session 8: Stigma, depression and wrap-up

OBJECTIVES

- Review the causes of, symptoms of and treatments for depression.
- Discuss stigma and mental illness.
- Discuss as a group what the participants learned about themselves and each other during the program.
- Have the participants complete the feedback form.

ACTIVITIES

1. Discussion: Stigma and depression
2. Activity: Beyond Girls Talk
3. Paperwork: Post-test/feedback and certificate of completion

MATERIALS AND HANDOUTS

- flip chart and markers
- food
- CD or mp3 player, and music
- pens
- Handout 8A: Post-test/Feedback
- Handout 8B: Certificate of Completion

Session 1: Introducing Girls Talk

OBJECTIVES

- Introduce the Girls Talk program and its goals, and give an overview of the eight sessions.
- Help the participants to get to know the other girls in the group.
- Fill out the required forms.
- Introduce the topics of mental health and depression.

MATERIALS AND HANDOUTS

- ☐ flip chart and markers
- ☐ food
- ☐ CD or mp3 player, and music
- ☐ bowl of Skittles
- ☐ journals
- ☐ stickers and other craft supplies to decorate journals
- ☐ pens
- ☐ Handout 1A: Program Schedule
- ☐ Handout 1B: Commitment Agreement
- ☐ Handout 1C: Pretest
- ☐ fact sheet "The Facts about Teen Depression" (available from www.mooddisorders.on.ca/pdf/TeenDepression_final.pdf)

RECOMMENDED RESOURCES

Non-fiction books

Scowen, K. (2006). *My Kind of Sad: What It's Like to be Young and Depressed.* Buffalo, NY: Annick Press.

> A guide to depression and its treatment for young people aged 13 and over; includes quotes from teens and an afterword by a youth psychiatrist.

Irwin, C. (1998). *Conquering the Beast: How I Fought Depression and Won—And How You Can Too.* New York: Three Rivers.

> The author shares her personal struggle with depression at age 14 and how she made her way back to health.

Guide

VALIDITY♀ team, CAMH. (2006). *Hear Me, Understand Me, Support Me: What Young Women Want You to Know about Depression.* Toronto: Centre for Addiction and Mental Health. Available: www.camh.net/Publications/Resources_for_Professionals/Validity/validity_eng.pdf. Accessed July 17, 2009.

The development of this guide was based on participatory research with young women regarding what they wanted service providers to know about depression, and includes personal stories from the young women.

Websites

Canadian Mental Health Association (CMHA)
   www.cmha.ca
   Provides a variety of information resources on depression and other mental health issues, and includes links to local CMHA branches.

Centre for Addiction and Mental Health (CAMH)
   www.camh.net
   Provides information on mental health and addiction and services available at CAMH.

Hearing Every Youth through Youth
   www.heyy.net
   A Toronto-based non-profit, volunteer-run organization that provides a telephone line for youth as well as links to youth websites and resources.

Kids Help Phone
   www.kidshelpphone.ca
   Provides telephone counselling for youth. The website has a variety of information resources on topics such as health, relationships, bullying and becoming an adult.

Mood Disorders Association of Ontario
   www.mooddisorders.on.ca
   Provides a variety of resources, including fact sheets on mental health issues.

Teen Mental Health
   www.teenmentalhealth.org
   Focuses on teens' mental health and provides information for youth, parents and community organizations. The website includes a blog, presentations and a list of books related to youth and mental health.

5 minutes

1. INTRODUCTION TO GIRLS TALK AND THE EIGHT SESSIONS

Information for facilitators

Though this information is primarily for the facilitators, you may share it with participants if it seems relevant.

Girls Talk is an eight-session program for girls between the ages of 13 and 16 that focuses on preventing and reducing the harm associated with depression.

The Girls Talk program has evolved as a part of a larger project called VALIDITY♀ (Vibrant Action Looking Into Depression In Today's Young Women), a participatory action research project aimed at gaining a better understanding of factors that lead to depression in young women, and developing strategies, materials and interventions to address these factors.

The main theme that emerged from this process was the need for a safe space where girls could be themselves and not have to deal with the unrelenting pressures of adolescence and daily life. Girls stressed the need for a supportive environment in which they could share their feelings with other girls without fear of negative comments or ridicule. They recognized that the stigma of mental illness is a huge barrier to getting help. They also described a need to strengthen self-esteem; to understand ways to develop meaningful relationships; to understand the influence of the media on young women; and to educate parents, teachers and service providers about depression and about how they can help.

Handout 1A

Information for participants

Distribute **Handout 1A: Program Schedule**, which outlines dates and topics for each of the eight sessions. Tell the participants:

There are eight sessions in the Girls Talk program. The topics we cover include stress, relationships (both dating relationships and relationships with friends and family), self-esteem, media, body image and stigma. The topic of depression will be discussed throughout the sessions as well as being the main focus of the final session. Each session will include a group discussion and an artistic or physical activity. At the end of each session you will have the opportunity to write in a journal if time permits, or you may take some time on your own to reflect on a topic from the session.

© 2009 CAMH

The journals will be used to reflect on each session, and the facilitators will give you topics to write about each week. To make sure that what you write stays private, you will take your journal home and bring it to each session. The journals are yours to keep at the end of the program and you will not be asked to share any information you write.

Explain the limits of confidentiality to the participants:

Any information discussed and collected during the sessions will be kept strictly confidential within the limits of the law. But if, for example, a participant tells us that she intends to harm herself or others, or that she or someone she knows under the age of 16 [in Ontario] is being harmed in some way, we must disclose this information to the proper authorities, and will also provide the participant with access to help.

Let participants know that help is available in case they or their friends need it. Have a local crisis support phone number available—you can write it on the flip chart.

2. ICEBREAKER: A LITTLE KNOWN FACT

15–20 minutes

Have the girls sit in a circle, if possible. Ask each participant to introduce herself to the group. As they do so, ask them to share a "little known" fact about themselves.

Depending on how the girls heard about the program, they may be wondering why they are participating. It may be helpful to have a discussion about why they think they are in the group or why they want to be in the group. Ask the girls what they think the program is about and why they are participating.

Reassure them that the program is intended to be a fun experience of learning and sharing with one another.

3. PAPERWORK: COMMITMENT AGREEMENT AND PRETEST

5 minutes

Handout 1B
Handout 1C

Distribute **Handout 1B: Commitment Agreement**, and ask the participants to fill out **Handout 1C: Pretest**. Explain the purpose of these forms. The commitment agreement is a way of formalizing their commitment to participate in the group, and the pretest is part of the evaluation of the Girls Talk program. Ask the girls to complete the commitment agreement at the end of the session, once they are more familiar with the group.

You may wish to play some music while the girls complete the forms. Let them know you will be putting the music on and ask them to bring music they would like to listen to while completing activities in the coming weeks.

15–20 minutes   ## 4. ACTIVITY: SKITTLES

The objective of the Skittles game* is for the girls to share information about themselves so they can get to know each other better. By the end of the activity the girls will probably feel that they have more in common with each other. The questions they have to answer allow them to focus on the positive parts of their lives rather than the negative.

- Explain that this is a fun activity to help the participants to get to know each other a bit better.
- Ask the girls to pass the bowl of Skittles around the circle.
- Ask each girl to take several Skittles and pass the bowl to the next girl (tell them not to eat the candies yet).
- After everyone has taken some candies, have each girl answer the questions below that correspond to the colour of her Skittles. It may be helpful to have these questions on a flip chart for reference.

Skittles questions

Red: What is something that makes you angry, and what can you do to resolve it?
Orange: What is the thing you are most proud of achieving?
Yellow: What do you like best about yourself?
Green: What is the best compliment you have ever received?
Purple: What is the best way you deal with stress?

* Source: Youth Net Halton. (2005). *Pens & Paints Program Manual*. Halton, ON: Author.

10 minutes

5. GROUND RULES

Ask the participants what ground rules they would like to see for the program. Write the rules on the flip chart and ask the girls to determine what the consequences should be if the rules are broken.

Display the ground rules in subsequent weeks as a reminder of what the group has decided.

It is important for the girls to determine their own ground rules, but make sure that the following rules are included:
• Keep confidentiality: a promise to keep what is said by others private.
• Respect each others' ideas and opinions.
• Let one person speak at a time.
• Have fun!

20–30 minutes

6. DISCUSSION: GIRLS' MENTAL HEALTH

What issues affect girls today?
• Allow the participants to have an open conversation about current stressful issues in their lives.
• Some examples may be stress about parents, school, friends, relationships, and so on.
• The purpose of the discussion is open sharing about the issues that are common to most of the girls in the group.

What is mental health?
• We all have mental health, just as we all have physical health.
• Mental health is the ability to feel, think and act in ways that help us to enjoy life and deal with the challenges we face.
• People can reduce their chance of emotional and physical health problems by learning how to cope with everyday life events and by making positive, healthy choices.
• When you are mentally healthy, you are able to have fulfilling relationships with people, adjust to change and make good decisions.
• Things that may negatively affect your mental health are social factors (e.g., lack of friends), physical factors (e.g., chronic illness such as diabetes) and biological factors (e.g., genes, hormones).

- Balancing the various parts of your life is important to maintain good mental health.
- The purpose of this discussion is to get a basic understanding of mental health.
- A definition of mental illness: "A disturbance in thoughts and emotions that decreases a person's capacity to cope with the challenges of everyday life" (CAMH, 2001).
- Examples of mental illness include depression, schizophrenia, eating disorders and anxiety disorders.

What is depression?

- It is normal to have ups and downs—everyone feels blue once in a while. But with depression, these feelings and symptoms last for a prolonged period and begin to interfere with normal activities.
- While there is no single cause of depression, some of the influencing factors include genetics, environment, distressing life events, biochemical imbalance in the brain, and psychological factors (such as a negative or pessimistic view of life).
- The main symptom of depression is a sad, despairing mood that is present most days and most of the day; lasts for more than two weeks; and impairs the person's performance at work, at school or in social relationships.
- People may experience depression in very different ways. For example, as well as a sad mood, they may experience physical symptoms such as upset stomach, headaches or body aches and pains.
- Depression can affect the way a person thinks and how his or her body acts.
- Share with the girls one or both of the following quotes from participants in the VALIDITY ♀ team's *Hear Me, Understand Me, Support Me* (2006, p. 7), expressing the challenges they experienced in identifying the signs of depression in themselves:

I think a lot of girls don't know the signs of depression. I didn't know I was depressed until, like, years after—and it was clinical depression too. I said to myself "No! Maybe I'm just sad today."

I probably could have been diagnosed with depression at the age of 14 or so, but I didn't understand what was going on—I just thought I was sad because of what was happening. It wasn't until I was out on my own that I had the time to really think about what was going on in my life, what I had been through and what I had to deal with.

- Ask the girls to name some of the feelings and behaviours they think are signs of depression. These might include some of the following:
  – grades dropping
  – having negative thoughts or feelings about yourself
  – taking more risks than you used to
  – withdrawing from friends and family
  – losing interest in things you previously enjoyed
  – having difficulty making decisions
  – having trouble concentrating
  – feeling irritable or angry
  – feeling helpless or hopeless
  – feeling anxious, nervous or restless
  – feeling sad or "down"
  – feeling guilty
  – experiencing a change in sleep patterns
  – feeling more tired
  – having thoughts of death or suicide.

- If you are having a few of these symptoms, you should talk to someone you trust—however, depression can only be diagnosed by a doctor or psychologist (in Ontario).
- If you are having thoughts of death or suicide, speak to someone you trust immediately.
- Depression can come after big changes in your life, such as moving, parents separating, or conflicts at home or with friends.
- Many people do not realize that they are depressed.
- According to CAMH's most recent report on the mental health and well-being of Ontario students (Adlaf et al., 2007), female students in grades 7 to 12 are significantly more likely than male students to report symptoms that put them at risk for depression (8.3 per cent versus 2.4 per cent).
- Distribute the fact sheet "The Facts about Teen Depression." Ask the girls to read the handout and share anything that they found surprising or that they were not aware of.

<table>
<tr><td>15 minutes</td></tr>
</table>

15 minutes

7. INTRODUCTION TO JOURNALS

Distribute journals to the participants. Ask the girls to decorate their journals using the craft supplies to make their journals unique to them. Remind them to bring their journals to each session.

Journal writing

Ask the girls to write for 10 minutes on the topic "My impressions of the first Girls Talk session":

- How did you feel coming to the group today (e.g., excited, nervous)?
- How do you feel now after participating in the group?
- What did you like best about today?

The girls may complete this activity in the session or at home, as time permits.

Program schedule

The Girls Talk program will be held every _____ for eight weeks.

Commences on: _____.
                   day   month   year

Place: _____

_____

_____

Time: from _____ to _____.

Weekly session topics

Week 1: Introducing Girls Talk

Week 2: Stress

Week 3: Relationships with friends

Week 4: Relationships with parents or caregivers

Week 5: Dating relationships

Week 6: Self-esteem

Week 7: Body image and the media

Week 8: Stigma, depression and wrap-up

Commitment agreement

I, _____, will commit myself to the eight-week Girls Talk program by giving my energy and my attendance.

I understand that I have the right to pass on contributing to discussions that might make me feel uncomfortable; however, I will be an active listener to support the other girls in the group.

Girls Talk mission statement

The Girls Talk program provides a safe place for girls to connect with each other and to learn about depression and its contributing factors. The participants will develop self-awareness, coping strategies and critical thinking skills though artistic and recreational activities.

Pretest

Date: _____ Age: _____ Grade: _____

Please indicate the extent to which you agree or disagree with each of the following statements by circling the appropriate number from 1 to 5.

		Disagree				Agree
1.	I am knowledgeable about mental health and mental illness in general.	1	2	3	4	5
2.	I know the possible causes of depression.	1	2	3	4	5
3.	I know about treatments and activities to help people with depression.	1	2	3	4	5
4.	I know about ways to improve my self-esteem.	1	2	3	4	5
5.	I know how stress can affect my body.	1	2	3	4	5
6.	I know what I can do to feel better when I'm stressed.	1	2	3	4	5
7.	I know the differences between healthy and unhealthy relationships.	1	2	3	4	5
8.	I am confident I can recognize some of the symptoms when I am feeling depressed.	1	2	3	4	5
9.	I am aware of the resources in my community that I can use if I'm having a problem.	1	2	3	4	5
10.	I know the names of adults in my school or community who I can talk to when I need to.	1	2	3	4	5
11.	People with mental illness are far less of a danger to others than people believe.	1	2	3	4	5
12.	The best way to handle people with mental illness is to keep them behind locked doors.	1	2	3	4	5

Session 2: Stress

OBJECTIVES

- Discuss different causes of stress.
- Teach healthy ways to cope with stress and have the participants share their own coping strategies.
- Have the participants learn how stress affects girls' bodies by sharing their own experiences.
- Help the participants to understand how depression can arise out of a stressful situation and times of transition.

MATERIALS

- ☐ flip chart and markers
- ☐ food
- ☐ CD or mp3 player, and music
- ☐ pre-drawn outlines of a body on paper (enough copies for girls to work in pairs)
- ☐ pens
- ☐ yoga mats, gym mats or towels
- ☐ DVD player and yoga instruction DVD (or guest yoga instructor)

RECOMMENDED RESOURCES

Guide

VALIDITY♀ team, CAMH. (2006). *Hear Me, Understand Me, Support Me: What Young Women Want You to Know about Depression.* Toronto: Centre for Addiction and Mental Health. Available: www.camh.net/Publications/Resources_for_Professionals/Validity/validity_eng.pdf. Accessed July 17, 2009.

Website

Kids Help Phone
  www.kidshelpphone.ca
  Provides telephone counselling for youth and information resources.

10 minutes

1. ICEBREAKER: STAND UP

Tell the participants that you will read some statements and that they should stand up if they agree with each statement or if it applies to them. Start off with an easy statement: "I brushed my teeth this morning." Then proceed to statements that may lead to discussion when the girls have stood up, such as:
• I like school.
• I have a brother or sister.
• I think stress is healthy for you.
• I have trouble talking to my parents.
• There are things in my life that really stress me out.
• I know someone who is depressed.
• I sometimes feel like nobody understands what I am going through.

Add or omit questions, depending on the group.

The objective of the activity is to let the girls see that they are experiencing some of the same things that other girls do. The exercise also helps the girls and facilitators get to know each other better.

15 to 20 minutes

2. DISCUSSION: STRESS

What is stress?
• Stress is the impact of an event or situation on your mind and body; these effects can be both beneficial and harmful.
• Stress is our response to change.
• Stress is any demand (force, pressure or strain) placed on a person and the person's response to it.

What are some things that "stress you out"? Is there something that happened today or recently that made you feel stressed?
• The purpose of this discussion is to have the girls relate to one another by realizing they are stressed by many of the same issues.

How can stress be positive?
• It can be a motivator to accomplish tasks.
• "Stressed" spelled backwards is "desserts."

What are some healthy and unhealthy ways to deal with stress?
- Have the girls brainstorm different ways in which they deal with stress, and have them label these strategies as healthy or unhealthy.
- Everyone has different ways to cope with stress; one way may be healthy for one person but unhealthy for another. An example is exercising: overall, exercise is very good for stress relief, but over-exercising can be unhealthy.
- Cutting may be brought up as a way to cope with stress. Emphasize the importance of learning other coping strategies beyond self-mutilation.

How do you think stress is related to depression?
- There is a complex relationship between stress and depression.
- Sometimes people will develop depression following a stressful event in their lives.
- Some people become depressed as a result of dealing with chronic stress—for example, living in an abusive home, putting too much pressure on themselves to succeed, or making major changes in lifestyle.
- The theory of "learned helplessness" argues that when people experience chronic stressful events, they learn to feel helpless. This feeling of helplessness is strengthened when a person believes they have no control over the situation.
- For example, if a student consistently does poorly in school, he or she may begin to feel that no amount of effort will help in achieving better grades; the person feels no control over his or her grades.

15–20 minutes

3. ACTIVITY: STRESS AND THE BODY DIAGRAM

Ask the girls to work in pairs for this activity. Distribute a pre-drawn body outline to each pair and invite them to label the areas of the body where they "feel it" when they're stressed out. Ask them to discuss with their partners what stress feels like in their body, and what some of the physical signs are when they are having a stressful time.

Bring the whole group back together and discuss their diagrams. If no one has labelled the head or brain, do so—this will reinforce the discussion about stress and depression.

Some of the ways in which stress can negatively affect the body are:
- acne
- increased blood pressure
- clenched jaw
- tight back, shoulders and neck
- indigestion
- nausea
- headache
- diarrhea.

30–40 minutes

4. ACTIVITY: YOGA DEMONSTRATION

Have a local yoga instructor do a demonstration of yoga poses and breathing techniques to teach the girls how to use yoga as a coping strategy. Alternatively, borrow a yoga instruction DVD from the local library and help to lead the girls in the poses yourself.

For this activity, you will need to bring a yoga mat or towel for each girl, or you can use gym mats.

15 minutes

5. JOURNAL WRITING

Ask the girls to address the following topics in their journals:
- How will you use what you have learned today in your daily life?
- If you were feeling sad about something, what are some ways you can make yourself feel better?
- What are your impressions of the second Girls Talk group?

Session 3: Relationships with friends

OBJECTIVES

- Review the signs of healthy and unhealthy relationships.
- Remind the participants that everyone has the ability to be a good friend.
- Discuss how relationships can affect mental health.
- Discuss anger within relationships.

MATERIALS AND HANDOUTS

- ☐ flip chart and markers
- ☐ food
- ☐ CD or mp3 player, and music
- ☐ scissors
- ☐ paper bag or other container
- ☐ small pieces of card, one envelope per girl
- ☐ healing bracelet supplies (beads, wire, etc.)
- ☐ pens
- ☐ Resource Sheet 3A: Personal Attributes
- ☐ Handout 3A: Colour Meanings and the Spectrum

RECOMMENDED RESOURCES

Articles and reports

Brown, L.M. (2008, March 5). *10 Ways to Move Beyond Bully-Prevention (And Why We Should)*. Available: http://hghw.org/docs/10ways_ew.pdf. Accessed July 20, 2009.

   This article provides tips on preventing bullying.

Krashinsky, S. (2009, March 30). What to do about cyber bullies? Get real, for a start. *The Globe and Mail*. Available: www.theglobeandmail.com/news/technology/article684977.ece. Accessed July 17, 2009.

   This newspaper article provides information about cyber-bullying and how it is different from other types of bullying, including personal stories and statistics.

Mishna, F., Wiener J. & Pepler, D. (2008). Some of my best friends—Experiences of bullying within friendships. *School Psychology International,* 29 (5), 549–573.
   This study provides an assessment of bullying situations among friends from the perspectives of the victims and their parents and teachers.

Van Daalen-Smith, C. (2006). *Living as a Chameleon: A Guide to Understanding Girls' Anger For Girl-Serving Professionals.* Toronto: York University. Available: www.camh.net/Publications/Resources_/for_Professionals/Validity/ Anger%20Research%20Monograph%20Final.pdf. Accessed July 20, 2009.
   This report, based on a doctoral dissertation, draws on interviews with 65 girls, conducted to better understand what generates anger, how they are allowed to express it and its relationship to depression.

Pamphlet

Girl Guides of Canada. (n.d.). *I Believe in We! Girls United: Challenges to Connect.* Available: www.midislandgg.com/documents/I-Believe-in-We.pdf. Accessed August 5, 2009.
   Provides bullying-related activities to do with girls.

Websites

Kids Help Phone
   www.kidshelpphone.ca
   Provides telephone counselling for youth and information resources.

Safe Canada
   www.safecanada.ca/topic_e.asp?category=28
   Provides information on bullying.

20–40 minutes

1. DISCUSSION: RELATIONSHIPS WITH FRIENDS

In order to have enough time to cover all the material in this session, you may want to consider having the girls work on this activity simultaneously with Activity 3. This may also help to put the girls more at ease while addressing sensitive topics.

What is a healthy relationship? What is an unhealthy relationship?

Write the participants' responses to these questions on the flip chart. Be sure to include some of the following qualities of healthy relationships:*

- *Communication*: Both people in the relationship need to feel free to express positive and negative feelings, complaints and affection.
- *Positive approach to conflict*: In all relationships there are times when communication breaks down; healthy relationships are able to manage conflicts and become stronger.
- *Shared expectations*: Both people need to be on the same page about what they want from the relationship.
- *Boundaries*: Both people need to be clear about what is OK and not OK in the relationship.

What are some qualities of a good friend?

- Qualities of a good friend include respect, consideration, loyalty (no backstabbing), tolerance and acceptance, support, sincerity, listening and understanding, honesty, sharing and generosity.
- It is important to both talk and listen (be an active listener).
- Active listening means that when someone is speaking, the other person listens closely, thinking about what is being said (without thinking ahead about what he or she is going to say in return) and repeating back key information to make sure he or she has understood the person correctly.

How do you think that a healthy or unhealthy relationship can affect a person's mental health?

- A healthy relationship can improve someone's mental health by letting them know there is someone understanding to talk to and confide in.

* Adapted with permission from State University of New York. (n.d.). *Maintaining Healthy Relationships* [Website]. Geneseo, NY: Author.

- A participant in the VALIDITY♀ team's *Hear Me, Understand Me, Support Me* (2006, p. 4) spoke about why it can be difficult to confide in friends: "I've spilled my guts to entire strangers on the street . . . And yet I can't reach out to my closest friends. I think it's because you're a lot more scared of how they'll judge and criticize you."
- According to CAMH's 2006 OSDUS (Ontario Student Drug Use Survey) report (Adlaf et al., 2006), four per cent of female students in grades 7–12 say they have no one to whom they can confide their problems.
- An unhealthy relationship can harm a person's mental health.
- There is a relationship between a person's perception of his or her social success and the person's self-esteem.
- The relationship between depression and self-esteem may be viewed as a vicious cycle. Not being able to connect with others in social situations may lead to low self-esteem and thus to depression, which in turn makes it harder still to connect with others.

What would you say about a girl who expresses her anger in public or toward a friend?

In discussing this question with the girls, refer to *Living as a Chameleon* (see the recommended resources for this session, page 38).

- There is a difference between anger and assertiveness.
- It is very common for girls and young women to suppress anger in relationships from fear of damaging a relationship with a friend or loved one by "rocking the boat."
- Women might suppress their anger for fear of people hurting them or becoming angry with them.
- Women may be labelled (e.g., as a "bitch") when they express their point of view—particularly if it goes against social norms.
- It isn't the fact that women get angry that causes depression, but the anger in combination with dismissal or disinterest by significant others that drive women to "self-silence."
- According to Simone de Beauvoir (cited in Pipher, 1994), "Girls stop being and start seeming."
- Women do not have a common language for anger and therefore it is harder to express.

What types of things make you angry in a relationship?

Most anger is derived from injustices, denied rights, abuse, harassment, dismissal, devaluation, denied agency and being made to feel unimportant and unappreciated. Examples include:

- not being allowed to do something because a loved one says so (for no other reason than for control)
- feeling that you are not being heard by a loved one
- being told that your opinions do not matter
- expressing concern and being told that you have no reason to feel that way
- feeling left out or isolated
- being called names or being bullied into something
- being the subject of rumours (rumours are often a source of hurt and anger among girls and young women, as they are a form of communication women frequently use to convey anger and "get back" at someone).

Why do you think girls have a tendency to be competitive with each other?

- Girls' treatment of other girls is a reflection of and a reaction to the way society treats them.
- Girls judge other girls because they are afraid of being judged themselves.
- The fear of rejection is very strong among girls, so they compete to keep their relationships.

What is bullying? What are some examples of bullying?

- Bullying often involves hurting someone who is weaker or less confident by repeatedly and systematically harassing or attacking them in some way.
- Bullying can be done by an individual or a group.
- Bullying can take many forms:
  - physical bullying: e.g., hitting, kicking, pushing, stealing or damaging property
  - verbal bullying: e.g., name-calling, threats, rude comments
  - social bullying: e.g., leaving people out from a group, spreading rumours or gossip, setting others up to look foolish
  - cyber-bullying: e.g., harassing or threatening through e-mail, text messages or websites.
- A participant in the VALIDITY♀ team's *Hear Me, Understand Me, Support Me* (2006, p. 38) speaks about her experience with bullying: "Sometimes, like in the lower grades, people make fun because others come from different

countries, they don't speak the same as everyone else, they have trouble speaking French because of the country they came from and their religion, how they dress—if they don't have a lot of money they can't dress well. You can see it starting even then, that people are making fun."

- According to Adlaf et al. (2007), 32 per cent of female students reported being bullied in the previous year.
- Cyber-bullying (or Internet bullying) is becoming a reality for an increasing number of young people.
- A survey by Kids Help Phone found that more than 70 per cent of respondents had been bullied online. In the cyber-world harm can happen faster and be more widespread.
- If someone is bullied online the harassment doesn't end when the person arrives home. A message can appear at any time on a cell phone or a computer screen.

What can you do if you are being bullied?
- Everyone has the right to be treated fairly and with respect, and to feel safe and included.
- You can say no to unwanted behaviour and you have the right to seek help from a trusted adult. Asking for help is about trying to find solutions to the problem.
- Think about how your behaviour may be making the problem bigger or smaller.
- Ignore the bullying and walk away, making them think you just don't care.
- Laugh it off—humour shows you're not bothered.
- Stay close to students you can count on to stick up for you.
- Stay away from areas where bullying tends to happen.
- Act confident, hold your head up, make eye contact and walk confidently.
- Make the time to do things that help you feel good about yourself.
- Be assertive, not aggressive. Fighting back can make things worse.

10 minutes

2. ACTIVITY: PERSONAL ATTRIBUTES

Resource Sheet 3A
Cut up **Resource Sheet 3A: Personal Attributes**, fold the individual words and put them into a paper bag or other container. The girls pass around the bag and each takes a piece of paper. In turn, they read out the word and share with the group how they think the word relates to healthy relationships.

20 minutes

3. ACTIVITY: GIVING COMPLIMENTS AND HEALING BRACELETS

In this activity the girls will have an opportunity to practise formulating and receiving compliments. Tell them that when they are stressed out, paying someone a compliment or doing something nice for others can help relieve their own stress. Compliments are a way of praising someone or showing appreciation and admiration for who they are as a person or for the things they do.

While it is good to give and receive all types of compliments, the ones that have the greatest impact are those that emphasize a person's abilities or good qualities. Provide the girls with examples of these types of compliments.

Write each girl's name on a separate card and place the cards in a bag or box. Ask each girl to select one card. Ensure that no one has her own name. The participants will do two things for the person whose name is on the card they have selected. First, each girl is asked to write a compliment for the person whose name is on the card she has chosen (e.g., "You are funny"). Tell the girls not to write superficial or "surface" comments (e.g., "I like your hair"), but rather ones that capture the person's abilities or qualities.

Handout 3A

Second, using the materials provided, each participant will create a healing bracelet for the same girl. Distribute **Handout 3A: Colour Meanings and the Spectrum** to help them choose colours for each others' bracelets (bearing in mind that the qualities represented by a given colour may vary between cultural contexts and groups). Once this is completed, the card and the bracelet are placed in an envelope with the girl's name on it and given to her to keep.

After the activity, have a brief discussion about why it is important to be able to accept a compliment.

20 minutes

4. ACTIVITY: STORYTELLING CIRCLE*

Arrange the chairs in two circles—an inner circle and an outer circle—so that each chair faces another chair in the other circle. Ask the girls to take a seat in one of the chairs. With music playing in the background, ask them to take turns telling the girl opposite about a time when they were *excluded* from a group. What was the exclusion based on? How did it feel?

Give them a few minutes for the discussion and then stop the music. Once the music stops the conversation ends, and everyone sitting in the inner circle moves one seat to the right. Ask the pair facing each other to now take turns telling each other about a time when they felt *included*. How did it feel? What was the feeling based on?

When the activity is over, ask the girls to share what they realized or learned from hearing and telling their stories. What was it like for them to tell their stories? Which was easier, telling a story of being included or of being excluded?

15 minutes

5. JOURNAL WRITING

Ask the girls to address the following topics in their journals:
- Is there a way you can deal positively with anger? How can you channel your emotions so they can help you instead of possibly hurting you or making the situation worse?
- Are there things in your life that you are angry about? If so, what are they and how do you show your anger?
- If you feel depressed, how can your friends help you feel better?
- If one of your friends is feeling depressed, how can you support her (or him)?
- If you saw another person being bullied, what is one thing you could do to help it stop?

* Adapted with permission from Hossfeld, B. & Taormina, G. (2005). *Friendship: 8-Week Facilitator Activity Guide.* Cotati, CA: Girls Circle Association.

Personal attributes

Confident	Courageous	Happy	Spontaneous
Gentle	Patient	Unique	Generous
Compassionate	Tolerant	Reasonable	Reliable
Empathetic	Giving	Helpful	Considerate
Brave	Nurturing	Non-judgmental	Supportive
Self-Aware	Calm	Peaceful	Loving
Optimistic	Trustworthy	Sensible	Understanding
Accepting	Wise	Concerned	Caring
Respectful	Positive	Sensitive	Loveable
Self-Accepting	Sincere	Assertive	Sharing

Source: Youth Net Halton (2005). *Pens & Paints Program Manual*. Halton, ON: Author.

Colour meanings and the spectrum*

The basic colours of the spectrum are the most fundamental colours: red, orange, yellow, green, blue, indigo and violet. These colours combine with each other and with white and black to create all of the other colours that we can see. The colour meanings of the basic light spectrum are summarized below (the information is based on Western colour meanings unless otherwise noted).

Red: The colour meanings of red include pleasure, desire, vitality, will to win, love of sports and the survival instinct. The "warm" colours red, orange and yellow are considered stimulating colours.

Orange: The colour meanings of orange are creativity, confidence, intuition, friendliness and the entrepreneurial spirit.

Yellow: The colour meanings of yellow are enthusiasm, cheerfulness, sense of humour, fun, optimism and intellectuality.

Green: The colour meanings of green are perseverance, patience, growth and healing. Green is also related to work, wealth and career.

Blue: The colour meanings of blue are related to freedom, strength and new beginnings. Blue skies mean optimism and better opportunities. Blue is cooling and relaxing. Blue symbolizes water, the source of life. Agricultural people have traditionally worshipped water in the form of rivers, clouds, mist and rain.

Indigo: The colour meanings of indigo are wisdom, self-mastery and spiritual attainment. Indigo has an inward rather than an outward orientation. Indigo connects the conscious and unconscious minds. Indigo should not be used for a person who is depressed, as it can also deepen negative moods.

Violet: The colour meanings of violet are the psychological quality of transformation, transmutation and the balance of power and love. Additional meanings include charisma, charm, magical abilities and tolerance.

* Adapted with permission from Karlsen, K. (2009). *Colors Meanings And Specific Colors* [Website]. Bozeman, MT: Author. Available: www.livingartsoriginals.com/infocolorsmeanings.html#spectrum. Accessed July 17, 2009.

Session 4: Relationships with parents or caregivers

OBJECTIVES

• Review the qualities of healthy relationships.
• Discuss the impact of relationships with parents or caregivers, with respect to depression.
• Teach ways to effectively communicate and maintain positive relationships with parents or caregivers.

MATERIALS AND HANDOUTS

☐ food
☐ CD or mp3 player, and music
☐ boxes (one for each participant), decorative materials, glitter, stickers, scissors, glue
☐ pens
☐ Handout 4A: Communicating with Parents or Caregivers
☐ Handout 4B: Using "I" Statements
☐ Handout 4C: Feelings List

RECOMMENDED RESOURCES

Websites
Kids Help Phone
   www.kidshelpphone.ca
   Provides telephone counselling for youth and information resources.

U.S. Department of Health and Human Services, Girls Health website
   www.girlshealth.gov
   Provides information on a variety of teen-related topics, including family relationships.

10 minutes

1. HEALTHY RELATIONSHIPS

Do you remember some of the qualities of a healthy relationship? How would it benefit you to be in a healthy relationship?
- Review the qualities of a healthy relationship discussed in Session 3.

What are some ways that you can communicate better with family members and everyone else in your life?
- Relationships with parents or caregivers are important and can sometimes be challenging too, especially for teenagers. Good communication is really important in relationships with parents or caregivers and with others.

Handout 4A

Distribute **Handout 4A: Communicating with Parents or Caregivers** and review the tips, providing examples where possible. Encourage the girls to keep the handout and to refer to it before talking to their parents or caregivers about issues that are important to them.

30–45 minutes

2. DISCUSSION: RELATIONSHIP WITH PARENTS

Start this discussion with the following excerpt of Katherine's story from the VALIDITY ♀ team's guide *Hear Me, Understand Me, Support Me: What Young Women Want You to Know about Depression* (2006, p. 10). This guide is based on research with young women regarding what they wanted service providers to know about when working with them. Explain to the girls that this story was written by a young woman named Katherine. They may find that they have had experiences similar to those that Katherine has had with her parents. There will be an opportunity to talk about these experiences in the discussion that follows.

Hear Me, Understand Me, Support Me also includes other first-person accounts by young women that you might find useful.

Katherine's story
My parents made a big impact on my views while I grew up. They had different pasts, different experiences. My father left to join the navy at 19 and my mother came to New Brunswick to start over from scratch since her degree in education was worthless in Canada. Both had dealt with racism and hardship coming into a new country. Thirty years later, there are times when they would say, "We're not

like them, we're different" or, "We're Vietnamese, not white." I'm not saying that they were hardcore, it's us against the world. But more like some people just cannot accept us the way we are, so we have to work hard to stay at the top. The top would be successful Caucasian men I guess.

Parents have such an influential role in our lives. There are some that are more adaptable and others who really value their religion and culture. Strict religions, like Muslim women who have to wear hijabs or Sikh men that wear turbans in public. They dictate values such as medical care and relationships, even the use of tampons. Some still value arranged marriages. The pressure of cultural expectations from friends, family and most importantly ourselves is a constant tug of war.

How would you describe your relationship with your parents? Can you relate to Katherine's story?

According to CAMH's most recent report on the mental health and well-being of Ontario students (Adlaf et al., 2006), 5.4 per cent of female students say they don't get along with their parents, while 27.5 per cent seldom or never discuss problems with their mother and 57 per cent seldom or never discuss problems with their father.

Are there times when your parents have a hard time hearing what you want to say?

Refer to **Handout 4A**.

What causes conflict with parents? Do differences in cultural values and beliefs cause conflict? Do you think conflict in your relationship with your parents can be positive?

- Causes of conflict can include curfews; friends; sex; alcohol and other drugs; changes in your role in the family as a young adult; and changes in values and beliefs.
- Conflict is a normal part of any relationship. As you get older, there are changes in the way you think, how you deal with your parents and how your parents deal with conflicts with you. Conflict can be looked at as giving and taking in the relationship.
- Open communication with parents can help you to navigate conflict, and help your parents to better understand and adjust to the new "emerging adult" that they have in the house.

- Sometimes anger and loud arguments are part of the conflict. Discipline is sometimes a consequence of parents' disagreeing with your decisions or behaviour. But if the arguments, punishments and yelling go too far, last too long or are too frequent, it can lead to stress and unhealthy consequences. Threats and intimidation, relentless criticism and frequent put-downs can erode a person's self-worth and are a form of emotional abuse. Teens who are abused often have trouble sleeping, concentrating or eating. Abuse is a common cause of depression in teens. Sometimes teens do not recognize that they are being abused because they have been treated that way for a long time and think it is normal. Abuse has no place in love. If you suspect a friend is being abused, encourage her or him to talk to an adult you both trust.

What can you do to build or maintain a positive relationship with your parents? What works?
- Demonstrate that you are trustworthy and responsible for what you say and do.
- Respect rules as much as possible and, when it is hard to do so, explain why.
- Understand that your parents grew up at a different time and perhaps in a different place or culture, and this may affect the way they see things.
- Keep lines of communication open with your parents. Tell them about every-day happenings and ask them about their day. This helps in maintaining connection and trust.
- Disagree without being disrespectful. Use respectful language and behaviour when expressing your opinions. Remember to use "I" statements to share your feelings (see below). Listen to your parents' point of view and avoid putting down their ideas and beliefs.

20 minutes

3. ACTIVITY: USING "I" STATEMENTS

Handout 4B
Handout 4C

Distribute and review **Handout 4B: Using "I" Statements** and **Handout 4C: Feelings List.** Have the group break into pairs. In turn, each girl in the pair creates an "I" statement to describe a feeling of her choice from the handout. She can make up what happened and imagine what she might want from the other person. Then she expresses the same feeling *not* using an "I" statement. Ask each of the partners to share with each other how it felt to share the feeling and to hear it expressed in both ways.

Return to the larger group and ask the girls how it felt to say and hear the "I" statements. How did they want to respond to the different statements? Can they imagine a situation when communicating with parents/caregivers or other significant people in their lives where "I" statements could be useful? Reassure the girls that although it may seem awkward to use this new way of communicating, with practice it will become easier and seem more natural.

10–15 minutes

4. ACTIVITY: MEMORY BOX

Have the girls decorate a "memory box." They can use this box to store pictures, stories and mementos that remind them of happy times with family and friends. Alternatively, they may want to give the box to someone special.

15 minutes

5. JOURNAL WRITING

- Write about a time when you and your parents communicated well. What made it good communication?
- What specific things can you and your parents do to improve or maintain a good relationship with each other?

Communicating with parents or caregivers

You may have found that your relationship with your parents is changing. There are a number of reasons for this. You are at an age when your body and mind are growing and developing. The teenage years are a time when you start to find your own solutions to problems, develop your own ideas on issues and begin to explore what you would like to do in the future. Some of these changes may make it more difficult for you to talk with your parents. You may find yourself arguing with them more than you used to.

Here are some tips that can help you to avoid arguments and approach sensitive topics with your parents.

Pick a good time: Try to pick a time when your parents are free to focus on what you have to say. Let them know there is something you would like to talk about and ask them if it's a good time to have a conversation or if they could tell you when they have some time to set aside to talk with you. There may be times when what you have to say is urgent. In this case tell them directly that there is something urgent that you need to discuss with them.

Look at them: It's easier to talk to someone when you look at the person. Looking at people when *they* are talking also helps you listen to what they are saying. Sometimes if we look away, we stop listening and instead start focusing on what we are going to say next.

Use a calm voice: Think about *how* you will say what you have to say. If you use a calm voice rather than yelling, it will make it easier for your parents to listen. Responding to your parents in a calm way and listening to what they have to say will show them that you are mature and responsible.

Say something nice first: Start the conversation with something pleasant or complimentary. You could also start by talking about everyday things.

Be clear—say what the problem or issue is and why it is so: Be direct in the language you use, and clearly identify the problem or issue at hand. Think about what you will say in advance of the conversation and, if it helps, write it down. Remember to use "I" statements to communicate how you feel and what you would like to happen.

Offer a solution: If possible try to offer a solution. Explain how it is possible and what the benefits might be of resolving the issue in the way you propose. Once you have agreed to a solution or a rule, stick to it. Show your parents that you are trustworthy and responsible.

Thank them for listening: Being respectful in the way you communicate with your parents includes thanking them for listening to you.

Using "I" statements*

With a partner, take turns to create an "I" statement using the emotion you have chosen from the **Handout 4C: Feelings List**. You can make up what happened and imagine what you might want in the situation. Then in turn, express the same emotion *not* using an "I" statement. Share with each other how it felt to express the emotion and to hear the emotion expressed in both ways.

1. Identify and state your feelings clearly. For example:
   - "I'm angry" (or irritated, enraged, upset).
   - "I'm hurt."
   - "I'm sad."
   - "I feel betrayed."
   - "I'm embarrassed."
   - "I'm lonely."
   - "I'm ashamed."

2. Use this basic formula

   When you said (or did) _____, I felt _____.

   What I want from you is _____.

   Here are some examples that demonstrate the use of I statements.

   When you didn't call, I felt _____, and I wanted you to _____.

   I heard you say _____ and I felt _____.

   I was disappointed when _____. I wanted _____.

* Adapted with permission from Girls Circle Association. (2002–2005). *Relationships with Peers: 10-Week Facilitator Activity Guide.* Cotati, CA: Author.

Feelings list*

Foolish	Disgraced	Silly	Awkward
Uncomfortable	Humiliated	Distracted	Confused
Abandoned	Miserable	Disappointed	Alone
Let down	Ignored	Rejected	Frightened
Worried	Afraid	Uneasy	Nervous
Overwhelmed	Enraged	Offended	Resentful
Annoyed	Infuriated	Frustrated	Disgusted
Troubled	Furious	Upset	Betrayed
Insulted	Cheated	Devalued	Forgotten
Intimidated	Neglected	Defeated	Put down
Oppressed	Helpless	Incapable	Inferior
Inadequate	Unworthy	Foolish	Uncomfortable
Distracted	Amused	Delighted	Fortunate
Soothed	Deprived	Glad	Proud
Excited	Ecstatic	Fabulous	Thrilled
Peaceful	Relieved	Grateful	Relaxed
Surprised	Thankful	Hopeful	Satisfied
Involved	Concerned	Curious	Confident
Optimistic	Energetic	Adventurous	Goofy
Delighted	Happy	Encouraged	Eager
Embarrassed	Refreshed	Motivated	Alive
Secure	Safe	Terrified	Indifferent

* Adapted with permission from Girls Circle Association. (2002–2005). *Relationships with Peers: 10-Week Facilitator Activity Guide.* Cotati, CA: Author.

Session 5: Dating relationships

OBJECTIVES

- Discuss the impact of dating relationships on self-esteem and depression.
- Teach how to identify unhealthy relationships and how to get help.
- Discuss decision making within dating relationships.

MATERIALS AND HANDOUTS

- ☐ food
- ☐ CD or mp3 player, and music
- ☐ stickers and markers
- ☐ tape and scissors
- ☐ pens
- ☐ Handout 5A: Power and Control Wheel
- ☐ Handout 5B: Equality Wheel
- ☐ Handout 5C: My Rights for Date Nights
- ☐ Resource Sheets 5A–5F: Dating Violence Facts

RECOMMENDED RESOURCES

Websites

VALIDITY ♀ project
  www.camh.net/validity
  A participatory research and development project where young women
  discuss their personal stories of depression.

Respect in Action (REACT)
  www.metrac.org/programs/info/speakers.htm
  Information about a peer education program, offered by Toronto's
  Metropolitan Action Committee on Violence against Women and Children
  (METRAC), that includes workshops and speakers.

Dating Violence—Say NO!
  www.phac-aspc.gc.ca/ncfv-cnivf/publications/rcmp-grc/fem-crimedat
  vio-eng.php

A website of the Public Health Agency of Canada that provides guidelines for what to do if you or a friend is in an abusive relationship.

Planned Parenthood Toronto
   www.ppt.on.ca
   A resource for sexual health information, including information for LGBTQ youth.

Sexuality News Bulletin
   www.sexualityandu.ca
   Provides current information on sexual health.

Supporting Our Youth
   www.soytoronto.org
   A program of Sherbourne Health Centre in Toronto that offers services, outreach and supports for LGBTT youth.

Teens Health
   http://teenshealth.org/teen
   Offers information on a variety of issues for teens and parents.

25–35 minutes

1. DISCUSSION: DATING RELATIONSHIPS

Is there pressure for youth to be in dating relationships? How could cultural attitudes and beliefs affect this?
- It is normal for teenagers to be interested in dating relationships.
- Because teens mature at different rates, some may be very interested in dating while others are not at all interested. Sometimes girls develop an interest in dating earlier than boys do.
- Friends and social groups can influence a teen's view of the importance of dating. Sometimes there is pressure to date because it is "what the cool or popular teens do."
- Some cultures view dating very differently. This puts teens in conflict as they try to fit in at school while obeying their parents' wishes and respecting their culture.

How would you define a healthy dating relationship?

- A healthy relationship includes mutual respect, trust, good communication, honesty, support, fairness and equality, and separate identities.

Do you think gender identity and interest in same-sex relationships affect a teenager's self-esteem? How?

- One participant in the VALIDITY ♀ team's *Hear Me, Understand Me, Support Me* (2006, p. 31) said:

In my fourth year of high school, I recall sitting in class and overhearing a conversation between two classmates that caught my attention: "Same-sex marriage is just wrong. It's sick and disgusting. Think about it, they're gonna start trying to make everybody else gay." From this conversation, rage consumed me and many questions formed in my head: What do you know about being queer? What's wrong with same-sex marriages? Why are you straight people constantly tearing us up?

- U.S. studies have found that gay, lesbian and bisexual teens are more likely to seriously consider and attempt suicide than heterosexual teens (Russell & Joyner, 2001; Faulkner & Cranston, 1998).

What is the difference between infatuation, sexual desire and love?

- Infatuation is an admiration or attraction stimulated by an appeal to our emotions.
- Sexual desire is a longing to be sexually involved with someone.
- Love is a powerful feeling of care and tenderness and includes a bond of mutual attachment and devotion based on understanding and trust and a sense of future.

How can you know the difference?

- Relationships take time to evolve. Sharing experiences, conversations and activities helps you to really get to know someone.

Do you think sex is viewed differently for girls and guys? Why?

- A study of high-school girls with boyfriends found that those with boyfriends three or more years older were more likely than girls with similar-aged boyfriends to engage in all forms of sexual intimacy, to have sex under the influence of alcohol or other drugs, and to experience sexual coercion (Gowen et al., 2007).
- An Australian study found that teenage girls who lose their virginity when they are not ready—often at an early age (median age 14)—are more likely to feel disappointed and regret the experience. The girls' decision making was influenced by peers, social expectations, needing to fit in, alcohol and wishing to keep their romantic relationships (Skinner et al., 2009).
- A study in England and Scotland found that overall 30 per cent of teens regretted their first experience of intercourse, with 19 per cent of girls feeling they were pressured into it and 10 per cent of boys feeling pressured (Wight et al., 2000).

How might low self-esteem affect dating relationships?

- Low self-esteem can lead to early sexual involvement, sexual promiscuity and unhealthy or abusive relationships.

If someone was thinking about having sex, what type of information do you think they would need to know and where would they get it?

- Before becoming sexually active, a young person should consider issues such as birth control and sexually transmitted diseases.
- Information is available from a public health nurse, a social worker, a family doctor or a sexual health clinic.

10 minutes

2. ACTIVITY: DATING VIOLENCE FACTS

Resource Sheets 5A to 5F

What is dating violence and how does it affect teenagers today? Post copies of **Resource Sheets 5A–5F: Dating Violence Facts** around the room. Ask the girls to form groups of two or three to visit each "station" and perform a stretch while they read the statistics on the wall. When the girls regroup ask them to comment on a statistic that they were either surprised by or that they felt was very significant.

25–35 minutes

3. DISCUSSION: UNHEALTHY OR VIOLENT RELATIONSHIPS

What are some potential warning signs that someone might be in a violent relationship?

Handout 5A
Handout 5B

Use **Handout 5A: Power and Control Wheel** and **Handout 5B: Equality Wheel** to stimulate discussion.

If a person's partner does any of the following, the relationship may have the potential to become violent:

- puts the person down or calls her or him names
- criticizes the person in front of others
- stops the person from seeing friends or doing things the person enjoys
- slaps, kicks or pushes the person
- touches the person when it is not wanted
- uses threats or coercion (e.g., threatens to end the relationship if the person does not agree with the partner, or threatens to commit suicide if the other person leaves the relationship)
- uses the person's money for his or her own purposes
- pressures the person to use alcohol or other drugs
- blames the person when she or he messes up or when things go wrong
- tells jokes or makes nasty remarks about the person's gender, religion or culture
- makes the person feel afraid to say no to sex
- forces the person into sexual activity that she or he is uncomfortable with.

What tactics are used by controlling partners?

Controlling partners may use the following tactics:

- **Coercion and threats:** e.g., pressuring for sex; threatening to commit violence, to leave, to commit suicide
- **Intimidation:** e.g., punching the wall, throwing a chair across the room, giving "the look"—the main message is that you could be next
- **Emotional abuse:** e.g., name-calling, humiliation, mind games—it's meant to destroy self-esteem and it does, leaving scars that are difficult to heal
- **Isolation:** e.g., taking away friendships and chances to be with other people, getting rid of people who might help you, expressing jealousy and defending it as a sign of love
- **Minimizing, denying and blaming:** e.g., saying it's no big deal, denying there is anything wrong, blaming you or other people for what is going on

• **Male privilege:** e.g., treating women like servants, making all the decisions, acting like "the boss," expressing sexist beliefs, attitudes and behaviours.

What can you do if someone you know is in an unhealthy or violent relationship?

• Be there. Listen without giving advice, unless it is asked for, and believe what she or he tells you.
• Many victims of abuse believe that it is their fault. They think they "asked for it" or don't deserve any better. Help them to understand that it is not their fault.
• Don't pressure your friend to break up with her or his partner, and don't put the partner down. This may drive your friend away from you when she or he needs you most.
• Acknowledge your friend's confused feelings. Don't tell your friend how she or he should feel. Recognize that it is still possible to love someone who hurts you.
• Encourage your friend to get help from an adult. Offer to help the person find a counsellor she or he can trust, and offer to go with your friend to meet the counsellor.
• Call a domestic violence hotline anonymously to find out what you can do to help your friend.
• Get written information on relationship abuse and share it with your friend.
• Don't make victim-blaming statements like "You're stupid to stay with him" or "Why do you let her treat you like this?" This will not help your friend.
• Don't ever place conditions on support—let your friend know you will offer support no matter what her or his decisions are.
• Allow your friend to make her or his own decisions, and respect those decisions even if you don't agree with them.
• Call the police if you witness physical violence.

20 minutes

4. ACTIVITY: MY RIGHTS FOR DATE NIGHTS

Handout 5C

Distribute **Handout 5C: My Rights for Date Nights**. Have the girls decorate their copies with markers, stickers, etc., while they discuss each statement.

15 minutes   ## 5. JOURNAL WRITING

Dating relationships:
- What is important for you to feel respected in a dating relationship?
- How can you effectively communicate your needs in a dating relationship?

Healthy and unhealthy relationships:
- Reflect on relationships in your life, and write about one aspect of a relationship that you think is most important, and why.
- Reflect on an important relationship in your life. Do you consider it healthy or unhealthy? Why?

Power and control wheel*

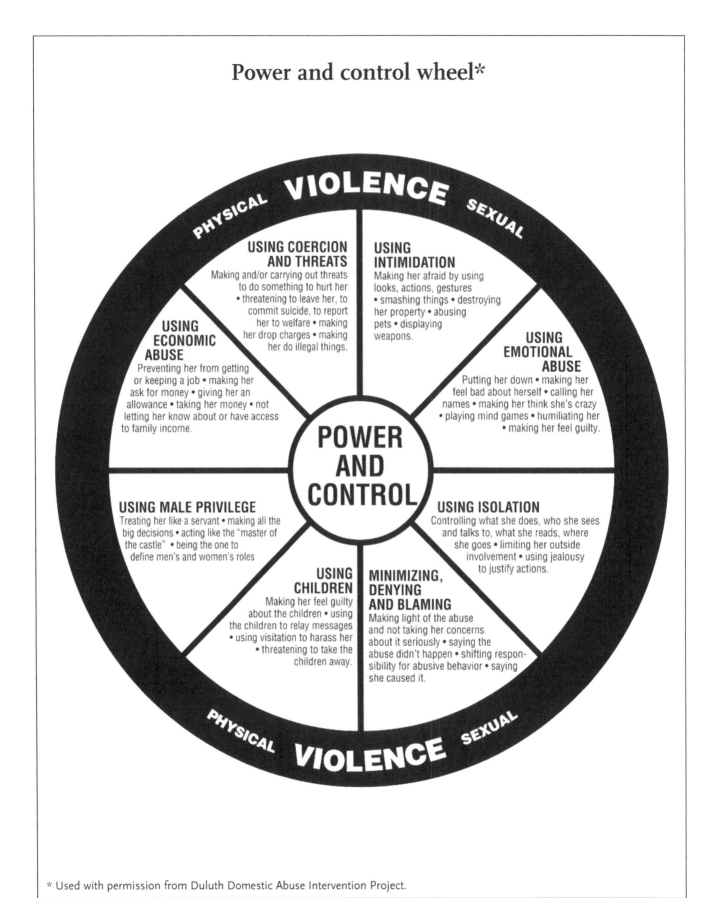

* Used with permission from Duluth Domestic Abuse Intervention Project.

Equality wheel*

NONVIOLENCE

EQUALITY

NEGOTIATION AND FAIRNESS
Seeking mutually satisfying resolutions to conflict • accepting change • being willing to compromise.

NON-THREATENING BEHAVIOR
Talking and acting so that she feels safe and comfortable expressing herself and doing things.

ECONOMIC PARTNERSHIP
Making money decisions together • making sure both partners benefit from financial arrangements.

RESPECT
Listening to her non-judgmentally • being emotionally affirming and understanding • valuing opinions.

SHARED RESPONSIBILITY
Mutually agreeing on a fair distribution of work • making family decisions together.

TRUST AND SUPPORT
Supporting her goals in life • respecting her right to her own feelings, friends, activities and opinions.

RESPONSIBLE PARENTING
Sharing parental responsibilities • being a positive non-violent role model for the children.

HONESTY AND ACCOUNTABILITY
Accepting responsibility for self • acknowledging past use of violence • admitting being wrong • communicating openly and truthfully.

NONVIOLENCE

* Used with permission from Duluth Domestic Abuse Intervention Project.

My rights for date nights*

I have a right:

to equality in relationships

to say "no" to physical closeness

to not be verbally or physically abused

to refuse a date without feeling guilty

to have my own interests and plans

to not act seductively for others

to set limits, say yes or no

to change my mind

to be me!

to express my feelings and tell others what I want or don't want

to choose to go places alone and not be paired up with someone

to have friends, including those of the opposite sex

to say, "I don't want to please you right now"

to say, "I want out of this relationship"

to say, "I love you" without sex

to say, "I don't want to do that"

to stop doing something even in the middle of doing it

to choose my own life goals and change them whenever I want to

to have my morals, values and beliefs respected

to say, "I need to know you better before I get more involved or have sex with you"

to discuss all my relationships confidentially with people in my life that I trust and respect

to put my own health and happiness first

to tell you when you treat me inappropriately or disrespectfully

to be loved for who I am and how I look and not be pressured to change.

* Adapted with permission from Girls Circle Association. (2002–2005). *Paths to the Future: 12-Week Facilitator Activity Guide.* Cotati, CA: Author.

Resource sheet 5A

Dating violence facts

In Canada, more than 50% of women experience at least one incident of physical or sexual violence after the age of 16 years.

Source: Status of Women Canada. (2002). *Assessing Violence Against Women: A Statistical Profile*. Report commissioned by Federal/Provincial/Territorial Ministers Responsible for the Status of Women. Ottawa: Author.

Resource sheet 5B

Dating violence facts

In Canada, less than 10% of sexual assaults are reported to the police.

Source: Statistics Canada. (2006). *Measuring Violence against Women: Statistical Trends 2006*. Ottawa: Author.

Resource sheet 5C

Dating violence facts

In one study:

- almost 50% of female high-school students had been emotionally abused

- almost 15% reported being physically forced into sex

- almost 10% reported being physically assaulted.

Source: DeKeseredy, W. & Schwartz, M.D. (1998). *Measuring the Extent of Woman Abuse in Intimate Heterosexual Relationships: A Critique of the Conflict Tactic Scales.* Harrisburg, PA: National Resource Center on Domestic Violence.

Resource sheet 5D

Dating violence facts

Girls and women between the ages of 16 and 24 are the most vulnerable to domestic violence, experiencing the highest rates of non-fatal violence from partners.

Source: Rennison, C.M. (2001). *Intimate Partner Violence and Age of Victim 1993–1999.* Washington, DC: U.S. Department of Justice.

Resource sheet 5E

Dating violence facts

Women under 25 are at highest risk for relationship violence, especially if they try to leave an abusive relationship. Young women are at the greatest risk for assault by intimate partners, and for spousal homicide and sexual assault.

Source: Status of Women Canada. (2002). *Assessing Violence Against Women: A Statistical Profile.* Report commissioned by Federal/Provincial/Territorial Ministers Responsible for the Status of Women. Ottawa: Author.

Resource sheet 5F

Dating violence facts

One study found that young women who had experienced depression were almost twice as likely than those who had not experienced depression to report experiencing moderate to severe violence from their partners as young adults.

Researchers concluded that young women with a history of depression in adolescence may be more likely to go on to develop relationships with high-risk partners.

Source: Lehrer, J.A., Buka, S., Gortmaker, S. & Shrier, L.A. (2006). Depressive symptomatology as a predictor of exposure to intimate partner violence among U.S. female adolescents and young adults. *Archives of Pediatrics and Adolescent Medicine, 160* (3), 270–276.

Session 6: Self-esteem

OBJECTIVES

- Through discussion and creative work, encourage girls to build healthy and durable self-esteem.
- Explore the power of words.
- Discuss factors that can affect self-esteem.
- Discuss how self-esteem is related to depression.

MATERIALS AND HANDOUTS

- ☐ flip chart and markers
- ☐ food
- ☐ CD or mp3 player, and music
- ☐ DVD player and dance instruction DVD (or guest dance instructor)
- ☐ pens
- ☐ cards, lettering and markers to make thank-you cards (if choosing this optional activity)

RECOMMENDED RESOURCES

Websites

Girls Only Interactive Self-Esteem Zone
   www.campaignforrealbeauty.ca/dsef07/t5.aspx?id=7987
   An interactive website exploring self-esteem and body image (note: this site is sponsored by Dove brand personal care products).

Real Me Experience
   www.realme.ca
   An interactive website of the National Eating Disorder Information Centre that allows girls to explore body image and related issues.

<table>
<tr><td>5 minutes</td><td>

1. ICEBREAKER: WHAT I LIKE ABOUT BEING ME

</td></tr>
</table>

5 minutes

1. ICEBREAKER: WHAT I LIKE ABOUT BEING ME

• Ask the participants to sit in a circle. Ask them in turn to describe one thing that they like about themselves that is not physical.

30 minutes

2. DISCUSSION: SELF-ESTEEM

What is self-esteem? What can affect your self-esteem?

• Self-esteem is how much you value or like yourself.
• Self-esteem can be adversely affected by unhealthy relationships with parents, friends, partners, teachers, coaches or others; unrealistic role models in the media; striving to be perfect; setting unrealistic goals; and constantly comparing yourself to others and looking to others for approval.

Why is self-esteem important?

• It helps you hold your head high and feel proud of the things you can do.
• It gives you the courage to try new things and the power to believe in yourself.
• It lets you respect yourself, even when you make mistakes.
• When you respect yourself, adults and your peers will respect you too.
• Having high self-esteem is having the power to hold true to your values. You will have the confidence to make good choices about your mind and body. When you have high self-esteem, you know you are smart enough to make the best choices for yourself.

What does it mean to value yourself?

• Get to know yourself better: listen to your real thoughts, feelings and needs. Ask yourself, "What is important to me?"
• Take time for yourself and do things that *you* value (not just what your friends, parents and others value).

How would feeling depressed affect your self-esteem?

- Depression in adolescents usually involves social and interpersonal difficulties which lead directly to self-esteem problems.
- As well as depression, other problems that tend to occur with with low self-esteem include unsafe sex, criminal activity and substance use problems.
- One participant in the VALIDITY♀ team's *Hear Me, Understand Me, Support Me* (2006, p. 27) said:

Personally, I know that grading myself against fashion supermodels made my self-esteem plummet, bringing with it my self-confidence, my sense of who I was, my feeling of self-worth, and ultimately my zest for life, my love for myself and my happiness, not to mention my health. I became clinically depressed on top of already having an eating disorder.

What can you do to build up your self-esteem?

- Love, respect and accept yourself.
- Learn to set realistic goals.
- Be forgiving of yourself and others.
- Honour uniqueness in yourself and others.
- Take care of your body, mind and spirit.
- Remember that you are more than your appearance.
- Be healthy and fit (not necessarily thin).
- Have meaning and purpose in life.
- Cultivate a sense of humour.
- Take pride in your cultural heritage.
- Feel safe and secure.
- Do good for others.
- Build your competence and achievements.
- Build a support system of family and friends.
- Value *your* needs, and prioritize taking care of yourself.
- Develop positive self-talk (see next page).
- Use positive affirmations (positive statements about yourself) to maintain a positive outlook.
- Learn to accept compliments with grace.

What is self-talk?

- Self-talk is the process of having an internal dialogue with yourself.
- It is a message we give ourselves automatically in response to our actions. This inner voice can either be our inner champion or our inner critic.
- Our self-talk can profoundly affect our self-esteem.
- Examples: When you make a mistake do you say, "Everybody makes mistakes" or "I am stupid?" When you succeed at something, do you think, "I did it!" or "I could have done better"?
- Negative self-talk is often intertwined with depression. Self-talk that leads to negative feelings and behaviour often occurs when:
  – our internal voice demands perfection and sees small problems as "failures"
  – we magnify our mistakes
  – we overgeneralize and say "I *always* fail" or "I *never* do anything right"
  – when we feel hopeless and say, "I could never do that."
- Practise changing your self-talk to be more forgiving, realistic and compassionate. Think of the qualities of a best friend. If your best friend constantly criticized you and never found anything positive to say, she or he wouldn't be your best friend for long. Your self-talk should be like a best friend.

15 minutes

3. ACTIVITY: INNER CRITIC VS. INNER CHAMPION

- Have the girls sit in a circle with their eyes closed, and read aloud the list* of "inner critic" statements below. Then, on the flip chart, record how the girls felt as the list was being read. Ask them how their bodies reacted. Next repeat the exercise with the list of "inner champion" statements. Given the emotional power of self-statements, this activity could lead into the journal writing activity on page 76.

Inner critic statements

I can't.
I have to.
I'm afraid to do it.
I'll fail.
I'm no good at it.
I can't do it.

* Used with permission from Girls Circle Association. (2002–2005). *Mind/Body/Spirit: 12-Week Facilitator Activity Guide*. Cotati, CA: Author.

I'm a loser.
I will never be happy again.
I am powerless to change this.
I'm dumb.
I'll never get it.
I'm not as good as the rest of them.
I am ugly.
I hate myself.
I always mess everything up.
I'm a jerk.
I can't do anything right.
I'll never make it.

Inner champion statements

I can.
I choose to, I want to.
I can try.
I'll succeed.
I am enough.
I can handle it.
I am special.
I will get through this hard time.
I can make a difference in my life.
I am smart.
I will get it.
I am me and I am great the way I am.
I am attractive.
I love myself.
I succeed often.
I am a nice person.
I can do many things well.
I can make it—I will try!

30–40 minutes

4. ACTIVITY: DANCING

- If possible, enlist the help of a local person who can teach the girls a few dance steps (e.g., hip hop, belly dancing or breakdancing).
- Alternatively, one of the girls in the group may have a background in dance and be able to lead to the group.
- Another option is to rent or borrow a dance instruction DVD.

20 minutes

5. ACTIVITY: THANK-YOU CARD (OPTIONAL)

- Give the girls materials to create a card to give to a friend or family member who makes them feel valued.

10 minutes

6. JOURNAL WRITING

Ask the girls to address the following topics in their journals:
- Write about one positive thing that you can do for yourself or someone else that could make a difference in your or their life? Explain how this action would make a difference.
- When you self-talk, what kinds of things do you say to yourself? If your self-talk is negative, what can you say to make it more positive? How could negative self-talk keep you from being the person you want to be or doing the things you want to do?

Session 7: Body image and the media

OBJECTIVES

- Encourage the participants to critically examine how the media portray young women and help create distorted ideas of body image.
- Examine the relationship between images in the media and self-esteem.
- Brainstorm ways to promote a healthy body image.
- Discuss the links between body image and depression.

MATERIALS

- ☐ flip chart and markers
- ☐ food
- ☐ CD or mp3 player, and music
- ☐ a selection of women's magazines
- ☐ bristol board (one piece for every two or three girls)
- ☐ scissors, glue, tape, markers
- ☐ computer with Internet connection (optional)
- ☐ pens

RECOMMENDED RESOURCES

Websites

About Face
   www.about-face.org
   Provides tools to resist and understand harmful media messages.

Body Image Coalition of Peel
   www.bodyimagecoalition.org/everybody1.html
   Provides information and an order form for *Every BODY Is a Somebody: Facilitators Guide*—a program to promote healthy body image, positive self-esteem, healthy eating and an active lifestyle for adolescent girls.

Dove Self-Esteem Film Gallery
   www.campaignforrealbeauty.ca/dsef07/t5.aspx?id=7985

Provides information and interactive tools to reinforce positive body image, including the time-lapse video "Evolution," which shows how computer-manipulated images distort our ideas of beauty.

Media Awareness
  www.media-awareness.ca
  Offers many articles on body image, media, self-esteem and the sexualization of girls.

National Eating Disorder Information Centre
  www.nedic.ca
  Provides information and resources on eating disorders and preoccupation with food and weight. A telephone information line is also available, providing information on treatment and support.

Real Me Experience
  www.realme.ca
  Interactive exploration of body image and self-esteem for girls.

The Student Body: Promoting Health at Any Size
  http://research.aboutkidshealth.ca/thestudentbody/home.asp
  A web-based training module, produced by Toronto's Hospital for Sick Children, to help teachers and other adults prevent unhealthy dieting in children.

30 minutes

1. DISCUSSION: BODY IMAGE AND THE MEDIA

What is body image? How would you define a healthy body image versus an unhealthy body image?

- Body image is the mental picture you have of your body. It includes your feelings and attitudes toward your physical appearance and also your perception of how others see you.
- People with a healthy body image accept and appreciate that healthy bodies come in a variety of shapes and sizes. They also recognize the positive attributes of their bodies. They are comfortable and satisfied with their body and would be critical of messages that focus on the ideal body.
- People with an unhealthy body image may be preoccupied with how they see themselves or with their perceptions of how others view them. They may be uncomfortable or unsatisfied with their body.

What can affect your body image?

- Body image can be influenced by friends (e.g., comparing weight, clothing sizes) or family members (being considered the "overweight" member of the family, having family members who focus on eating or their weight).
- Evidence suggests that friendship groups that focus on physical appearance have a negative influence on the body image, eating and exercise behaviours of those in the group.
- The pressure that our society puts on girls to be perfect causes many girls to react by, for example, overeating, undereating, exercising too little or too much, or other detrimental behaviours.
- The influence of the media has a powerful influence on girls' and womens' body image.

What are examples of the forms of media that influence us and why do we use them?

- In our society, we use a wide range of media—including broadcast media (e.g., radio, television), Internet, print media (e.g., newspapers, magazines), recordings, advertising and movies—to:
  - access information
  - relax
  - be entertained
  - escape
  - experience things outside of everyday life
  - sell things
  - communicate with others
  - know what is happening in our communities and the wider world.

What pays for mass media?

- Advertising dollars pay for the programs, messages and entertainment that we use. Advertisers market products by targeting our weaknesses and vulnerabilities.

How do you see women portrayed in the media?

- Common stereotypes include women who are portrayed as being extremely thin, with an unrealistic "hourglass" body shape, disproportionately large breasts, and "perfect" hair, skin, makeup and clothing. They are often either passive or controlling, either sweet and innocent or bitchy. They may be family oriented, sexualized, dependent on men, relationship focused, and obsessed with hair, fashion, makeup or cleaning products. They are often victimized or disempowered. Women are typically portrayed as being either desirable, young and thin or undesirable, fat and old. Whatever their ethno-racial background, female models' features tend to look Caucasian, or are sexualised and made to look exotic.

How do women's images in the media affect someone's body image and self-esteem?

- Girls and young women often try to compare themselves to the "perfect" images that are depicted in the media—which are unattainable. Most of these images are not realistic, since they are computer-generated or touched up.
- A girl's self-esteem can be harmed if in her "self-talk" she consistently compares herself to these images.
- The stress and frustration of trying to mould yourself to an impossible body standard can lead to very negative thoughts and beliefs about yourself (your self-esteem).
- Portrayal in the media as being valued only for their appearance and as objects of sexuality can lead girls and women feel powerless.

Negative body image can lead to unhealthy eating and weight manipulation. What does this mean?

- Unhealthy eating patterns and other ways of manipulating weight include restrictive, excessive and/or chaotic eating and exercise regimes.
- Healthy eating is always good for our bodies. But dieting is often *un*healthy, as it focuses on weight loss for appearance's sake rather than for health and well-being. Healthy eating and physical activity can encourage people to reach their healthy weight.
- Body shape and size are inherited. One study suggests that for females, genetics account for 77 per cent of body size and shape (Herskind, 1996).
- Parents' dieting encourages children to diet.
- Dieting can lead to eating disorders, but they are not the same thing.

- Eating disorders such as anorexia and bulimia are classified as mental illnesses.

How can you have a healthy body image?

- Know that beautiful women come in many shapes and sizes.
- Understand that beauty comes from the inside: the glow of confidence, the enjoyment of being connected to family and friends, or whatever is meaningful to you.
- Focus on your positive attributes and the things you *can* control.
- Start exercising and eating more fruits and vegetables—you'll feel better just changing these little things in your life.
- Don't believe everything you see. Start to recognize the images you see in the media for what they are: often constructed, manipulated and unreal.

How are images manipulated?

- Even models that many people see as "ideal" are not good enough for commercial purposes. What the media doesn't tell us is that women who are portrayed as having attained such perfection don't truly exist. Before publication, models' photographs are sent to labs for retouching, airbrushing and digital manipulation. Wrinkles are removed, waists are slimmed down, acne is erased, hair is shined and colour is added to the skin tone. Through creating these idealized images advertisers gain customers for life, because we are all encouraged to strive for what is impossible.
- Many relevant articles can be found at www.media-awareness.ca, along with media and Internet education resources for teachers and parents. The website www.psychcentral.com includes an informative article entitled "Minding the Media: The Latest Round of Photoshopped Celebrities."

30 minutes

2. ACTIVITY: MAGAZINE COLLAGE

As a whole group, have the girls create a "graffiti page" on chart paper, expressing what it means to be a girl.

Then, in groups of two or three, have half the girls create a collage by cutting out magazine pictures (at least five) that portray women in a negative way and sticking them on bristol board. Ask the remaining girls to create a collage of at least five positive portrayals. Each group should give its display a title and write a caption for each image.

Finally, lead a group discussion on the different messages and compare them to the graffiti page.

35 minutes

3. ACTIVITY: CHALLENGING NEGATIVE MEDIA MESSAGES

There are several good websites that encourage girls to take an active role in challenging the media's harmful messages. One excellent site that can be used to encourage advocacy is www.about-face.org. It critiques current advertisements and provides lists of the 10 worst offenders and the best positive advertisements. It provides addresses of the perpetrators and sample letters to make it easy to respond to the advertisers. Have the girls review the website and, in small groups, choose either a negative or a positive advertisement, and then work together to create a response to mail to the company. (If there is no Internet access at the location where the group is held, this can be a take-home activity).

15 minutes

4. JOURNAL WRITING

Ask the girls to address the following topics in their journals:
• What is your definition of a beautiful woman?
• In what ways do you compare yourself to others? How does this affect your self-esteem? How can you make changes to limit how much you compare yourself to others?
• What are some things you can tell yourself when you see unrealistic images of young women in the media?

Session 8: Stigma, depression and wrap-up

OBJECTIVES

- Review the causes of, symptoms of and treatments for depression.
- Discuss stigma and mental illness.
- Discuss as a group what the participants learned about themselves and each other during the program.
- Have the participants complete the feedback form.

MATERIALS

- ☐ flip chart and markers
- ☐ food
- ☐ CD or mp3 player, and music
- ☐ pens
- ☐ Handout 8A: Post-test/Feedback
- ☐ Handout 8B: Certificate of Completion

RECOMMENDED RESOURCES

Teens Health
  www.kidshealth.org/teen
  Includes many useful articles on mental health and therapy.

Canadian Mental Health Association
  www.cmha.ca
  A useful website for information on mental health for teens and adults.

Centre for Addiction and Mental Health
  www.camh.net
  Provides information, resources, publications, online tutorials and information on getting treatment.

30–45 minutes

1. DISCUSSION: STIGMA AND DEPRESSION

What is stigma?

- Stigma is a negative label attached to, for example, mental illness. It refers to negative attitudes (prejudice) and behaviour (discrimination) toward people who possess any attribute, trait or disorder that our society deems undesirable and shameful.
- We often label people for what they do rather than for who they are. For example, many people may label someone with depression as *being depressed*, instead of thinking about who the person really is as a whole, and seeing the depression as just one (often temporary) aspect of the person.

What do you do if someone calls you a name or gives you a label?

- Instead of letting someone get you frustrated, try to shrug it off or laugh.
- Remember not to let the labeller decide how others see you and you see yourself.

Is it fair to judge a group of people based on the actions of just a few?

- Ask the girls to close their eyes and in your best dramatic voice, read the following passage.*

> On ordinary streets, there is a disaster waiting to happen. There is a group of people among us who pose a threat to their neighborhoods and indeed to the whole community. Too often their potentially dangerous behaviour is ignored until it is too late. The public is angry about the alarming number of incidents in which *blondes* injure or kill innocent people. Hardly a day goes by without news of a murder or attack by a *blonde* leading many to question why they are allowed to live freely in the community. Even if, as some critics claim, it's only a small minority causing the problem, it's not always possible to know which *blondes* are dangerous. We must put the right of the community first and keep *blondes* in secure but humane institutions for their own good as well as ours.

*Source: Centre for Addiction and Mental Health. (2005). *Beyond the Label*. Toronto: Author.

Tell the girls to open their eyes, and ask them how they felt about the reading. Make the point that the reading reflects how people with a mental illness are often portrayed.

What are the effects of stigma?

Stigma can result in:

- a person hiding her or his problem and not seeking help until it has become much more serious
- a person having difficulty making friends, getting a job, continuing with school or participating in many activities
- negative feelings about oneself
- social isolation
- depression
- suicide.

What can we do to reduce the stigma that people with a mental illness such as depression face?

- Talk about mental health problems and learn the facts so you can understand people better.
- Realize that over 25 per cent of the population experience a mental illness over their lifetime.
- Don't shut out your friends who have mental health problems, but stand by them and talk to them. Understand that they need you—support systems are one of the most important factors that help people with a mental illness to get better. For teenagers, friends are an important resource.
- Be respectful of differences.
- Don't label people based on their mental health problems (people are more than just a disorder).

Review: What is depression and what may cause someone to become depressed?

- It is normal to have ups and downs—everyone feels blue once in a while. But with depression, these feelings and symptoms last for a prolonged period and begin to interfere with your normal activities.
- While there is no single cause of depression, some of the influencing factors include genetics, environment, distressing life events, biochemical imbalance in the brain, and psychological factors (such as a negative or pessimistic view of life).

- The main symptom of depression is a sad, despairing mood that is present most days and most of the day; lasts for more than two weeks; and impairs the person's performance at work, at school or in social relationships.
- People may experience depression in very different ways. For example, as well as a sad mood, they may experience physical symptoms such as upset stomach, headaches or body aches and pains.

Refer to the discussion in Session 1 for more information about depression.

What are some ways to treat depression?

Treatments for depression include:

- psychotherapy—also known as talk therapy—which may include cognitive-behavioural therapy (helping to change negative self-talk), interpersonal therapy and others
- art or creative therapy, which aids self-awareness through artwork created during sessions
- peer counselling
- medication (antidepressants), which is not always necessary but is often used if depression is severe, persistent and affects a person's functioning
- electroconvulsive therapy (ECT), which is only used rarely, when a person has severe symptoms and cannot take or does not respond to antidepressants; an electric shock causes the brain to have a seizure, changing the brain chemicals that regulate emotions.

What can you do if you start to feel depressed?

- Talk to a friend.
- See your family doctor or another health professional (e.g., a counsellor).
- Eat healthy foods—be good to your body.
- Participate in activities that make you feel better.
- Practice yoga or other physical activities that you enjoy.
- Try not to take on too many activities or tasks at the same time; break things down into manageable goals.
- Use positive self-talk.
- Let your family and friends help you.

What are your feelings about depression and people with mental illness now that you have participated in the Girls Talk program?
- This is a chance for the girls to talk about how the Girls Talk program has given them information about depression, mental illness and stigma.

45 minutes

2. ACTIVITY: BEYOND GIRLS TALK

Have the girls get into groups of three or four and brainstorm ways in which they can use the information they have learned in the Girls Talk program. They should report back to the group after 10 minutes of discussion. The facilitators record ideas for future Girls Talk groups.

10–15 minutes

3. PAPERWORK: POST-TEST/FEEDBACK AND CERTIFICATE OF COMPLETION

Handout 8A

Distribute copies of **Handout 8A: Post-test/Feedback** to each participant, and have them complete the form and return it to the facilitators.

Handout 8B

Distribute **Handout 8B: Certificate of Completion** to each participant and thank them for their active participation in the program.

Finally . . . celebrate!!

Post-test/feedback

Date: _____ Age: _____ Grade: _____

Please indicate the extent to which you agree or disagree with each of the following statements by circling the appropriate number from 1 to 5.

		DISAGREE				AGREE
1.	I am knowledgeable about mental health and mental illness in general.	1	2	3	4	5
2.	I know the possible causes of depression.	1	2	3	4	5
3.	I know about treatments and activities to help people with depression.	1	2	3	4	5
4.	I know about ways to improve my self-esteem.	1	2	3	4	5
5.	I know how stress can affect my body.	1	2	3	4	5
6.	I know what I can do to feel better when I'm stressed.	1	2	3	4	5
7.	I know the differences between healthy and unhealthy relationships.	1	2	3	4	5
8.	I am confident I can recognize some of the symptoms when I am feeling depressed.	1	2	3	4	5
9.	I am aware of the resources in my community that I can use if I'm having a problem.	1	2	3	4	5
10.	I know the names of adults in my school or community who I can talk to when I need to.	1	2	3	4	5
11.	People with mental illness are far less of a danger to others than people believe.	1	2	3	4	5
12.	The best way to handle people with mental illness is to keep them behind locked doors.	1	2	3	4	5

To make sure we're offering a program that young people enjoy, we would like your feedback to help us improve the program. Your answers will be kept **confidential**.

Please indicate the extent to which you agree or disagree with each of the following statements by circling the appropriate number from 1 to 5.

	DISAGREE				AGREE
1. Talking about my experiences helped me feel more connected to other girls.	1	2	3	4	5
2. Listening to other people talk about their experiences helped me feel more connected to other girls.	1	2	3	4	5
3. The discussions helped me to realize that other girls experience many of the same issues I do.	1	2	3	4	5
4. The program is a safe place to express emotions and feelings.	1	2	3	4	5
5. The program helped me to develop coping strategies.	1	2	3	4	5
6. I plan to use the coping strategies I developed when I feel stressed.	1	2	3	4	5

6a. If you developed some coping strategies that seem to work for you, please list them:

_____

_____

_____

7. I would recommend the Girls Talk program to a friend.	1	2	3	4	5
8. Overall, I enjoyed the Girls Talk program.	1	2	3	4	5

9. What was your favourite activity in the Girls Talk program?

_____

10. What was your least favourite activity in the Girls Talk program?

_____

11. Do you have any additional comments about the program?

_____

_____

_____

Thank you for your feedback!

CERTIFICATE OF COMPLETION

camh
Centre for Addiction and Mental Health
Centre de toxicomanie et de santé mentale

_____

(Participant's name)

We thank you for your energy and participation
in the Girls Talk Program

_____

(School or organization) (Date)

_____
Girls Talk Facilitator

_____
Date

_____
Girls Talk Facilitator

_____
Date

camh

Centre for Addiction and Mental Health
Centre de toxicomanie et de santé mentale

CERTIFICATE OF COMPLETION

We thank you for your energy and participation
in the Girls Talk Program

_____
Girls Talk Facilitator

_____
Girls Talk Facilitator

_____
Date

_____
Date

References

Adlaf, E.M., Paglia-Boak, A., Beitchman, J.H., Wolfe, D. (2006). *Detailed OSDUS Findings: The Mental Health and Well-Being of Ontario Students 1991–2005.* Available: www.camh.net/ Research/Areas_of_research/Population_Life_Course_Studies/OSDUS/OSDUS2005_ mental_detailed_fnl.pdf. Accessed September 3, 2009.

Adlaf, E.M., Paglia-Boak, A., Beitchman, J.H., Wolfe, D. (2007). *Detailed OSDUHS Findings: The Mental Health and Well-Being of Ontario Students 1991–2007.* Available: www.camh.net/ Research/Areas_of_research/Population_Life_Course_Studies/OSDUS/OSDUHS2007_ MentalHealth_Detailed_Final.pdf. Accessed July 17, 2009.

Centre for Addiction and Mental Health (2001). *Talking about Mental Illness: A Guide for Developing an Awareness Program for Youth. Teacher's Resource.* Available: www.camh.net/ education/Resources_teachers_schools/TAMI/tami_teachersall.pdf. Accessed July 17, 2009.

Faulkner, A. & Cranston, K. (1998). Correlates of same-sex sexual behaviour in a random sample of Massachusetts high school students. *American Journal of Public Health, 88,* 262–266.

Gowen, L.K., Feldman, S.S., Diaz, R. & Yisrael, D.S. (2007). A comparison of the sexual behaviors and attitudes of adolescent girls with older vs. similar-aged boyfriends. *Journal of Youth and Adolescence, 33* (2), 167–175.

Herskind, A.M. (1996). Sex and age specific assessment of genetic and environmental influences on body mass index in twins. *International Journal of Obesity, 20,* 106–182.

Pipher, M. (1994). *Reviving Ophelia: Saving the Selves of Adolescent Girls.* New York: Ballantine.

Russell, S.T. & Joyner, K. (2001). Adolescent sexual orientation and suicide risk: Evidence from a national study. *American Journal of Public Health, 91* (8), 1276–1281.

Skinner, R., Smith, J., Fenwick, J., Fyfe, S. & Hendriks, J. (2009). Perceptions and experiences of first sexual intercourse in Australian adolescent females. *Journal of Adolescent Health, 43* (6), 593–599.

VALIDITY ♀ team, CAMH. (2006). *Hear Me, Understand Me, Support Me: What Young Women Want You to Know about Depression.* Toronto: Centre for Addiction and Mental Health. Available: www.camh.net/Publications/Resources_for_Professionals/Validity/validity_eng.pdf. Accessed July 17, 2009.

Wight, D., Henderson, M., Raab, G., Abraham, C., Buston, K., Scott, S. et al. (2000). Extent of regretted sexual intercourse among young teenagers in Scotland: A cross sectional survey. *British Medical Journal, 320,* 1243–1244.

Appendix: Queen D

Young women wrote this section during a writing weekend in October 2004. This advice—in response to common questions about depression ("Queen D") —is from the young women themselves, not from health professionals.*

BY KATHERINE

Q: My friend is showing symptoms of depression. She doesn't like talking about the issue and I think she is in denial. How can I help her?

A: The first thing would be to make sure that she has a caring and supportive system around her. Obviously you are concerned about her, and making sure she understands this is very important. Tell her that you've noticed these symptoms and you're simply worried about her. Make sure that you don't pressure her and understand that she is very likely to avoid help for the first few tries. The crucial part would be to make sure that she doesn't feel labelled and different from anyone else. Depression is a serious illness that can be helped. Let her come to you when she is ready and then take it from there.

There is a possibility that she may not identify with depression but is going through something else. Make a list of questions to ask her about parents and things going on in her life. Questions like: "How are things in your relationship?" or "How are things in school?" or even "Have you been eating lately?" If worst comes to worst and things aren't improving, and she has come to a point where she is causing self-harm, then stepping in is a must. Tell someone in authority and that you both trust, like parents or a teacher. Basically, remember that she can only help herself. The best part you can play is to be there for her for support.

* This section comprises general information, and is not intended to diagnose or treat any health problem or disorder, or to be a substitute for informed professional advice.

BY TANYA

Q: My friends and I drink on a semi-regular basis. Some people say we have substance abuse problems, some say we have depression. Do I have a problem?

A: According to the 2003 *OSDUS* [*Ontario Student Drug Use Survey*] study, 64.3 per cent of female grade 7 to 12 students in Ontario have consumed alcohol.

There are many ways we can look at whether you are experiencing problems with depression or with alcohol, or both. First of all, we have to look at how much you drink and how often you drink. According to the 2003 *OSDUS*, binge drinking is identified as having five drinks or more on one occasion. Their findings show that 23.8 per cent of grade 7 to 12 females had experienced binge drinking in the four weeks being surveyed.

A second important factor that must be considered is the reasons why you're drinking. Are you drinking because your friends are drinking? Or because you want to drink? Or are you trying to escape from problems? I know that, from personal experience, I didn't think I had a drinking problem. It wasn't until I finally moved out of the house that I finally realized that my drinking was a problem. Not that I went out often or drank often, but it seemed that every time I did go out, there had been a fight or an argument at home within that past week and I just needed to forget about it. I would go out with my friends, get hammered, have a great time, and forget my problems for those few hours. I was considered a binge drinker. I remember one summer, I was living at home and an argument broke out between my dad and I, so I moved out. After living with a family friend for about a month, I decided to try going back home. Those were probably two of the most stressful weeks I had experienced, which landed me in the bar just about every night. I decided then that I couldn't be depending on alcohol to escape, because in the long run it would only make things worse—and I ended up moving back out of the house.

If you feel that your drinking isn't a problem, but you are still having feelings of being sad or angry, you may be experiencing feelings of depression. If this is the case, try talking to a doctor, going to a clinic or seeing a counsellor to discuss your problems. However, if you are more concerned that it may be a drinking problem, try looking into a support group such as AA. Another factor that might indicate you may have a drinking problem is asking yourself whether or not friends and/or family members are approaching you or talking to you about your drinking. Look for questions or comments such as "Seems like you've been drinking a lot lately," "Missing school [or work] again?" or "How about we do something else that doesn't include alcohol?" Always remember that whatever the problem may be, there are resources available. Try surfing the net for local resources or searching the phone book, or call Kids Help Phone at 1 800 668-6868 and talk to them about your problem and ask for local resources.

BY TIANA

Q: I have recently been feeling depressed. Is there any daily routine I can follow that would help deal with depression better or in a more organized way?

A: There is really no organized way to deal with depression. Since depression lacks consistency it's difficult to track your feelings down in a way that you can deal with them without help. If you are not comfortable with seeking help right away (don't worry, most people aren't) then take some time for yourself. If you want to, try writing in a journal. Sometimes writing down your emotions helps you to get organized or organizes your thoughts, confusions and the ways you feel overwhelmed. If writing isn't one of your strong points and you still do not want to see anybody about your feelings, try to clear your head, walk for 20 to 30 minutes a day, take time for yourself and your thoughts. If you're confused or overwhelmed or even angry, this is a great way to relieve stress. Also, exercising increases your serotonin levels. Which means some of the "not-so-great" feelings you might be having may get better with exercise. Keep yourself active if you can, but if you really don't see any results dealing with it on your own, I encourage you—as someone who has experienced dealing with depression (maybe not the same as you, though)—that it does eventually feel good to talk to someone (counsellor, therapist, friend, parent, sibling, teacher, etc). Because unless it's what you want, depression is not something you have to deal with alone.

BY MEAGAN

Q: I am a young girl, and have a lot of media influence in my life. I feel like I am being bombarded with images of the "perfect woman." When I can't live up to these standards, I feel like I've failed somehow and that I am worthless. Is there anything I can do to get past these feelings of depression?

A: As a female adolescent myself I can relate to the stress of feeling like you have to live up to the standards that the media puts forward. The media does an incredible job of selling products to young women by making them feel that in order to be accepted by society, they have to fit a certain image. Even being educated about the media and telling yourself not to let it affect you, doesn't help get those images out of your head. One thing to do is keep telling yourself these images aren't real. Be critical of everything you see and hear. These images are manufactured in a studio somewhere where they edit and airbrush them to look a certain way. The girls in the magazines have professionals doing their make-up, hair and wardrobe for the purpose of selling an image. The important thing to do is not to buy into it. Find out what your interests are and what you can do to be active in your community. If you join a sports team, act in a play, become a member of a social organization, you will not place such emphasis on how you look. Doing something you love, and being beautiful on the inside, is much more important than fitting into someone else's image of beauty.

BY SHAUNA

Q: I'm concerned that my daughter, who has been diagnosed with depression, is physically hurting herself. I'm really worried and I just don't know what to do to support her. Please help me help my daughter—I don't want her to do anything really serious to herself.

A: Dear concerned parent, first off let me assure you that you are not alone in everything that you are seeing your daughter experience as well as everything that you are experiencing as her parent. Self-harm behaviour can be a symptom of depression as well as a coping strategy for it. There are numerous reasons that your daughter could be hurting herself, such as being a way of self-nurturing, feeling like she needs to punish herself, changing emotional hurt (which is sometimes not easily dealt with) into physical hurt (which can be easier and less confusing), and even as a way of communicating to you that she needs help because something is wrong. However, no matter what the reason, it's crucial that you not ignore the issue, avoid it or brush it off as a minor thing. You need to talk to your daughter and find out how she is hurting herself in as much detail as possible: how is she hurting herself, with what, how often, for how long has it been going on, etc. But it will also be important to know that your daughter may not feel comfortable discussing the matter with you because the causes of their self-inflicted harm are often very confusing, and it is normally a behaviour that evokes a tremendous amount of guilt and shame and so would tend to be concealed.

Although it will undoubtedly be very difficult to talk about and confront your daughter on this topic, it must be done. If you just don't feel comfortable doing that, then you need to arrange for your daughter to see a therapist or doctor. If, however, you do feel comfortable broaching the subject, then know that most young women would prefer having very straightforward and very blunt questions asked, rather then feel like somebody who is trying to talk to them about a very difficult subject is walking on eggshells and is very uncomfortable. If you ask questions such as, "Have you been hurting yourself?" or "How have you been hurting yourself?" or (if you think that she is experiencing urges to hurt herself) "Do you want to hurt yourself?", then you are more likely to get a very direct answer and avoid some tension.

There are numerous ways in which a parent can support a child who is struggling with depression and self-harm behaviours, and having that support can play a significant role in overcoming depression and other negative behaviours. First of all, if you notice your daughter is having a really strong low period in her mood and could possibly be experiencing self-harm urges, then don't leave her alone. Suggest an activity that you can do together, such as watching a movie or going shopping. Not only will this be a way for you to ensure that your daughter is safe, but it can also serve as a distraction from the triggers. Any physical activity is also a great way of coping because it will produce endorphins, which are also produced when somebody self-harms, and will give her that same "high" without all of the negative effects. Another thing that often helps young women deal with self-harm, particularly with self-punishing and negative thoughts, is to write down all of the negative thoughts on half of a piece of paper, and then write a counter-positive thought on the other half of the paper. If your child is already seeing a therapist, then bring the self-harm behaviour to the therapist's attention so that together they can explore the causes as well as positive coping strategies. Lastly, know that the absolute best way that you can support someone going through depression is by being a safe haven for her to express and admit to her feelings; someone who will be non-judgmental, who they feel understands them, and who they can trust to be discreet. If you become this person for your daughter, then you are arming her with the strongest shield possible to fight her depression and other issues with. Remind yourself and your child that depression can be beaten, and don't lose hope or faith that she will overcome it.

Lightning Source UK Ltd.
Milton Keynes UK
UKOW07f1119171115

262912UK00016B/496/P